BECC

MW00616342

THE

EVERYDAY

ETHICIST™

DOING THINGS THE RIGHT WAY
THE FIRST TIME

An Ethics Guide for Individuals, Leaders, and
Organizations with an Introduction to
Total Ethical Auditing™ for Internal Auditors

AMANDA JO ERVEN, CPA, CIA, CFE

FOUR ACES PRESS
DENVER, CO

Becoming The Everyday Ethicist™

Copyright ©2020 by Amanda Jo Erven

For information about permission to reproduce selections from this book or license for use in a training program, contact Jo@AuditConsultingEducation.com

www.auditconsultingeducation.com

Four Aces Press
Denver, CO

Becoming The Everyday Ethicist /Amanda Jo Erven

1st edition

ISBN 978-1-7337843-4-4

THIS BOOK DEDICATED TO:

Every "whistleblower" and "tattletale" out there.

Thank you for speaking up.

Ethics do matter.

Character matters.

*"If you are faithful in little things,
you will be faithful in large ones.
But if you are dishonest in little things,
you won't be honest with greater responsibilities."*
– Luke 16:10 New Living Translation

Becoming The Everyday Ethicist

CONTENTS

PREFACE:

INTRODUCING THE TATTLETALE

IF YOU ARE READING this book, you must have an interest
in ethics and morality, and, hopefully a desire to live a more
ethical life. If you have read other books on ethics, you likely
have noticed that they were mostly written by academics in the
fields of philosophy or behavioral psychology. Philosophers
seem to focus on the history of great philosophical thinkers *(the
likes of Aristotle)* and they interpret and sometimes attempt to
apply the thoughts and concepts to current times and issues.

Psychologists focus more on behavioral ethics and attempt to explain conduct through experiments and other studies.

Other ethical content authors come from a religious, faith-based background or a self-help, personal development genre. In addition, it seems that all personal, professional, and leadership development books contain at least some information on the importance of character, ethics, integrity, and honesty.

I am not a philosopher or a psychologist, a religious leader or a self-help guru. But I am a churchgoer and part-time college professor that has been a whistleblower *(okay, a tattletale)* since birth. *(I mean, just look at the picture on the previous page.)* Admittedly, I have a passion for ethical behavior that some people cringe at. But those are most likely the "some people" that need this book the most.

My path to writing about ethics may have started at birth, but it truly materialized when I shifted from in *insider* to an *observer* of "Corporate America." I am a Certified Public Accountant (CPA), a Certified Internal Auditor (CIA), and a Certified Fraud Examiner (CFE), that has seen the "inside" of many companies, and, unfortunately, the "inside" of many leaders that also need to read this book.

> *"What is needed is a realignment of societies' priorities, where honesty and integrity are more important than fame and fortune."*
> – Joseph T. Wells

I believe my perspective on ethics is a little different than the philosophers, psychologists, religious leaders, or self-help writers, as they may not have had first-hand encounters with corporate cultures or (un)ethical leadership.

Regardless, I wanted to make sure you knew what you were getting when you picked up this book, and you understood why someone with a financial/auditing/fraud background would write a book about ethics. So, here's just a little bit more about me.

My professional education is in accounting, bachelor's and master's degrees, from the University of Georgia *(go dawgs!)*. Directly after, I began my career with a Big Four accounting firm as an Audit and Advisory Services Associate. I quickly moved from external auditing *(reasons to be divulged later)* to internal auditing, and ultimately to the position of Internal Audit Director with a large, international financial services company.

Subsequent to my corporate career, I founded my own firm, Audit. Consulting. Education. LLC *(hence the mention of the shift from insider to observer)*. As an "expert observer," I now provide internal audit strategy and independent risk, governance, process, control, and culture recommendations to organizations in almost every industry. *Side note:* Although I consider myself an *observer* now, I am treated like an *insider* by my clients, a fact that I pride myself on, very much.

I have also spent the past few years developing and perfecting my innovative concept of internal auditing called Total Quality Auditing® (TQA), based on the successful, proven Total Quality Management (TQM) principles by W. Edwards Deming. While traditional internal audit focuses primarily on historical data collection, analysis, and reporting, TQA focuses on future changes to culture, behavior, and processes necessary to meet organizational and customer needs for risk management and operational improvement.

My first book, *Total Quality Auditing: How a Total Quality Mindset Can Help Internal Auditors Add Real Value,* outlines six points of focus for improving the *real* value added by internal audit. *And guess what?* The first point of focus is ETHICS. *Why?* Because I strongly believe that ethics *(honesty, integrity, character)* is the cornerstone of controlling risks. The first thing internal auditors should work on is ensuring individuals, leaders, and organizations do the *"right"* things. If the ethics is not right, then other efforts of the organization will suffer and fail. And yes, there are plenty of examples that prove this point.

Since the development of the TQA concept, much of my energy has been spent on the education and training of audit and accounting professionals. And, as a by-product of the training, my general interest in ethics has developed and increased.

My second book, *Our Choices on the Road of Life (Second edition: Your Road. Your Choices.),* is a self-development book. It also has six points of focus *(i.e., "choices")* including, not surprisingly, a chapter on ethics called *"Choosing Impeccable Character."* The focus on character building emphasizes the importance of integrity and honesty in creating a fulfilling life and successful career. And because of how well this *"choice"* was received, I expanded my consulting and education offerings to include *"choices"* and *"ethics"* corporate and association training programs and keynote presentations.

So, since *personal* ethics is such a critical component for individual development and *cultural* and *leadership* ethics is foundational to organization success, it is only natural that my third book is purely focused on doing things the right way, the first time... on *Becoming The Everyday Ethicist.*

> *"With word and deed we insert ourselves into the human world, and this insertion is like a second birth...."*
> – Hannah Arendt

WHAT'S TO COME IN *BECOMING THE EVERYDAY ETHICIST?*

Overall, this book has three main "slices" that will outline many concepts on which to base 1) *personal* ethical conduct, 2) ethical *leadership*, and 3) an ethical *organization* culture. Oh, and it ends with a "bonus section" around ethical auditing *(remember, I am an auditor).*

The first chapter, *Introducing The Everyday Ethicist,* defines some of the terms associated with ethics and will begin to define what it means to be *The Everyday Ethicist.* We review some examples that help frame the ethical issues of today and establish some guidelines for ethical behavior that can be applied personally, in leadership roles, and to organizations in general.

The second chapter, *The Ethical Mirage,* reviews the findings of research in the area of behavioral psychology. The published studies of distinguished professors, researchers, and authors including Dan Ariely *(The [Honest] Truth About Dishonesty),* Sissela Bok *(Lying: Moral Choice in Public and Private Life)* and Eugene Soltes *(Why They Cheat)* will be referenced throughout the chapter. The critical questions are: *Why are people sometimes dishonest and exhibit unethical behavior? Why does evidence point to the fact that our society is not getting any better (and may be declining) ethically?* We find out very quickly that all evidence points to the fact that we are not as honest and ethical as we think we are – *The Ethical Mirage Proposition.*

The third chapter, *Ethical Anchors*, provides evidence, historical and current, for *"anchoring"* our behavior on sound ethical concepts and principles. Brief reference will be made to the works of the great philosophers of all time as well as my favorite, more contemporary, stalwarts of ethical thoughts and actions including Ken Blanchard, Norman Vincent Peale, John C. Maxwell, Jon M. Huntsman, John C. Bogle, David Brooks, Sissela Bok, and Michael J. Sandel. You will get to know a bit about each in the process of building – *The Ethical Anchor Proposition.*

The fourth chapter, *Ethical Choices*, draws a comparison and describes distinctive characteristics of individual ethical *(and unethical)* character choices. We explore the concept of *The Big Me,* introduced in David Brook's book, *The Road to Character.* Then we examine the characteristics of, what I call, *The Ethical Rationalizer* and understand why some can easily, consciously or unconsciously, rationalize away unethical behavior. Finally, we learn the characteristics of *The Everyday Ethicist* and lay the foundation for – *The Everyday Ethicist Proposition.*

> *"There is no witness so terrible or no accuser so powerful as the conscience."*
> – Sophocles

The fifth chapter, *The Everyday Ethical Leader*, deals with leadership characteristics and thoughts of great ethical and moral leaders of the 20th and 21st centuries. I lean on the lives, thinking, and benchmark leadership examples set by John C.

Bogle, Ben Horowitz, S. Truett Cathy, Bill George, W. Edwards Deming, and the many *Women of Ethical Leadership*. Again, you will also get to know each and the way they think. At the end of the chapter, I describe my ideal leader through – *The Everyday Ethical Leader Proposition*.

The sixth through tenth chapters are all about *organizations* and why some act ethically and others do not.

Chapter six starts with an identification of characteristics and thought processes of *(un)ethical organizations* – from the *"deny, deflect, deceit"* approach to the *"let's break everything"* mentality. If the goal is to run an (un)ethical organization, this provides the formula to do so – *The (Un)Ethical Organization Proposition*.

Chapter seven explores the various models of capitalistic enterprises along with the pitfalls of the traditional shareholder model. The pitfalls are explained, and I offer a non-traditional model *(The Inverted Stakeholder Pyramid Mindset inspired by A. A. Peck and Sons – a story about my step great-grandfather)* for promoting ethics in an organization – *The Ethical Organization Stakeholders and Priorities Proposition*.

Chapter eight describes the ethical conduct framework – establishing core ethical values and strong standards defining the boundaries of ethical conduct, as well as outlining the enforcement necessary to ensure ethical conduct throughout the organization – *The Ethical Organization Values, Standards, and Enforcement Proposition*.

Chapter nine is structure and process focused and identifies features necessary to promote and sustain ethical conduct in an organization. Subjects include hiring processes, training, communications, performance and compensation management, incentive systems, and feedback mechanisms to support ethical conduct – *The Ethical Organization Processes Proposition.*

Chapter ten pulls it all together summarizing the thinking, priorities, values, processes, and controls necessary to sustain an ethical culture full of everyday ethicists and ethical leaders – *The Everyday Ethical Organization Proposition.*

Last but not least, chapter eleven is about auditing and introduces a new term – Total Ethical Auditing™. It seems that all too often, ethical crises occur and everyone asks, "Where were the auditors?" Well, sadly, I believe auditors are too often working on the wrong things or working on things with the wrong approach. This chapter outlines processes for Total Ethical Auditing – TEA – auditing with ethics in mind. It will show internal auditors how to assess ethical risks or "red flags" of unethical conduct, by "planning and thinking like a fraud examiner." Then it will provide tips to "execute like an investigative journalist" and "mitigate like a coach." Lastly, it will show you the qualities of ethics, competence, skepticism, grit, and courage that auditors need to fulfill – *The Total Ethical Auditor Proposition.*

I have sprinkled the book with case studies, stories, and comments about past and current events relating to personal ethics, leadership ethics, and organization ethics. I hope the examples will highlight the relevance and importance of ethics in our society today.

And to further stimulate thoughts about ethics, you may have already noticed I include many of my favorite ethics-related quotes within. These are from people of all backgrounds who have been thinking, researching, and writing about ethics for a long time. Like John C. Maxwell, who said,

> *"Living an ethical life may not always be easy,*
> *but it need not be complicated."*

Now begins your journey to living an ethical life and Becoming The Everyday Ethicist. I truly hope you enjoy the ride!

Chapter One:

Introducing The Everyday Ethicist

THE HOUSTON ASTROS MAJOR league baseball team uses a video camera to steal catchers' signs to gain an unfair advantage and to win a World Series. Many players and coaches are all in the scheme. No one says anything until it is too late.

Desperate parents participate in scandals to falsify records and pay bribes for the unfair admission of their children to prestigious colleges and universities. Admission personnel and athletic coaches willingly participate.

Airbnb facilitates member hosts in an elegant scheme to avoid taxes, violate homeowner association ordinances and community regulations, and put travelers' health and welfare at risk. Some individuals notice, but most don't seem to care.

Social media companies seemingly do anything *(including gathering the personal data of children without parents' consent)* to sell private data to advertisers. Securing and protecting confidential user data has become far less important than peddling it to the highest bidder.

Doctors and hospital administrators overlook alarming spikes in death rates at the Johns Hopkins Children's Hospital in St. Petersburg, Florida. They take no initial corrective action until a journalist sends up a red flag.

Boeing is quick to shed responsibility and blame others for the crash of two Boeing 737 Max airplanes killing all passengers and crew. Boeing later grounds the planes, replaces the CEO for mishandling the crisis, and acknowledges that software design flaws were the cause of the crashes.

Thousands die of opioid drug overdoses each year but opioid manufacturers, distributors, prescribers, and dispensers, for the most part, turn a blind eye and accept no responsibility for the deaths. They deny, deflect, and deceive.

Then there are the huge ethical and moral lapses within the Catholic Church. And, for many reasons, perhaps including ethical ones, a 2018 Gallup poll reported church membership has declined by 20% in the previous twenty years.

And lastly and most recently *(literally as I am writing this book)*, U.S. Senators that seek a personal and financial advantage by trading stocks based on non-public, confidential national security information related to the 2020 coronavirus pandemic. Proving it's not just the letter of the law that's important; it's the spirit and intent.

> *"Judgments must be based on what is right and necessary and not on what people say and do."*
> – Leo Tolstoy

To me, each of the examples *(and, sadly, I could have gone on)* raise extreme ethical and moral issues and question where our priorities are as a society. I mean... bribes to obtain unfair advantages... financial rewards that trump safety concerns... profits being valued more than lives... personal greed over the social good. And, I haven't even mentioned the well-publicized scandals or fraudsters like Enron, Bernie Madoff, or the many players within the 2008 financial crisis.

So, what exactly is wrong with our personal and professional individual ethics today? What is wrong with our leaders' ethics? And what is wrong with our organizations' ethics? Why do some seemingly no longer care about being ethical in our everyday lives?

> *"Live by yes and no – yes to everything good, no to everything bad."*
> – William James

WHAT *IS* AN EVERYDAY ETHICIST?

Let me tell a story about by son, Benjamin. When he was in the first grade, his teacher asked the kids to write and draw *"doing the right thing."* Benjamin drew the above picture with a tree and a squirrel *(and admittedly some ginormous acorns)* and wrote *"when a squirrel is falling, cach [catch] it."* Okay, Benjamin gets high marks for thoughtfulness, not so much for spelling.

Now Benjamin may have seen a squirrel flying through the air once or twice, but I doubt that he ever caught one. I don't think he spent much time thinking about what to do if he were to come face to face with a falling squirrel, nor do I think he thought much about his motivations for or the consequences of catching the squirrel. But he instinctively thought that catching the squirrel was the *"right"* thing to do.

> *"We become just by doing just actions."*
> – Aristotle

What do Aristotle and Benjamin have in common? Since my son was six at the time, I guarantee he had not yet studied Aristotle's teachings. But it seems they both see the world in the same way: *"Do the right thing"* = *"Do just actions."*

Now in my opinion, Benjamin is a typical youngster, from a typical American family, going to a typical public school, surrounded by typical school mates and friends. So, how did Benjamin come to the conclusion that the *"right"* thing to do was to catch the squirrel?

My intuition says it came from watching his family, observing his teachers, and even from playmates on the playground and in the neighborhood. My theory is *"doing the right thing"* comes naturally early in life, long before the complexities of life enter the picture.

Or perhaps it's just easier to be an Everyday Ethicist when you are seven? Let's check out a few more examples.

> *"Keep true, never be ashamed of doing right, decide on what you think is right and stick to it."*
> – George Eliot

WHO *IS* AN EVERYDAY ETHICIST?

In 2005 in Afghanistan, Navy Seal Marcus Luttrell and other special forces' members deployed on a mission in enemy territory. He and his fellow soldiers came upon three local sheep herders. The soldiers instinctively knew that their cover could be blown if they let the herders go. Yes, they did consider their option of killing the sheep herders but made the decision to let them go unharmed *"even if"* they were to die as a result of their actions.

Soldiers did die. *So, did the soldiers do the right thing?*

> *"Ethics is doing the right thing when the act will cost more than we want to pay."*
> – Michael Josephson

I write about Archie Peck, Ralph Steinman, and Harriet Tubman in my book, *Our Choices on the Road of Life.* All three, at completely different times and places in history, made *"even if"* decisions out of respect for the lives and welfare of others.

Archie Peck, my step great-grandfather was a Medal of Honor recipient for his bravery and valor in World War I. While serving as an infantryman in the U.S 77th Army Division, his unit found itself surrounded by Germans and heavy enemy fire. In the bloody battle that ensued, Archie risked his own life to save two wounded fellow soldiers. *Did Archie do the right thing in risking his life for others?*

Ralph Steinman, a Canadian physician and medical researcher passed away from pancreatic cancer in 2011. While under treatment for his own cancer, he *"was so engrossed in his cancer vaccine research that he developed and tested an experimental treatment on himself."* Did Dr. Steinman do the *right thing in risking his life for a vaccine?*

Have you seen the 2019 movie *"Harriet"* about Harriet Tubman's life? If not, surely you remember her from the Civil War section of history class. Tubman was born into slavery in 1822. She was a civil war scout, spy, nurse, and later became a civil rights activist. She risked her life and freedom to guide a raid that led to the liberation of more than 700 slaves. *Did Harriet Tubman do the right thing in risking her life for liberty?*

The soldiers in Afghanistan, Archie Peck, Ralph Steinman, and Harriett Tubman each risked their lives to save lives. They were the examples of *The Everyday Ethicist* in their moment of history.

> *"Ethics is a code of values which guide our choices and actions and determine the purpose and course of our lives."*
> – Ayn Rand

THE EVERYDAY ETHICIST IN (SIMPLE) ACTION

I recently observed a young immigrant family checking out with items at a small sole proprietor grocery store. It was clear that the family had no knowledge of American currency and had no idea how much to pay. I watched as the proprietor meticulously counted out the money ensuring that the correct amount was paid for the items. The proprietor clearly was an Everyday Ethicist.

I once watched my father's retired men's tennis group in *"action" (if you could call it that)*. It was immediately obvious that they cared about one another, always making sure that if there was doubt about a line call, the call was made in favor of the opponent. The balls were courteously returned to the server and there were a lot of *"good shot"* comments made throughout the match. In the minds of the participants, there were no *"bad shots."* They kept score but no one seemed to care about it. At the end of the match, there were fist bumps all around. *Yes, first bumps.* They were playing the game with total respect for one another. A whole bunch of Everyday Ethicists in their own way.

Kids on the playground normally have an instinct *(learned or otherwise)* to cheer for those who make a good play, help someone who is hurt in the action, share toys *(hopefully)*, play games fairly and by the established rules. And when they do these things, they are little Everyday Ethicists.

An Everyday Ethicist calls attention to a $2 mistake on a restaurant bill, a $20 missed item while checking out at a Walmart, or a $5,000 error on a home closing statement *regardless* of who wins or loses in the transaction. *"Even if"* the loss is theirs.

> *"Character is how you act when no one is watching."*
> – Jon M. Huntsman

Everyday Ethicists don't fudge on financial statements, exaggerate expense reports, or steal even $1 from the petty cash drawer.

Everyday Ethicists don't cheat on tests and they return lost wallets and purses *(more later)*.

Everyday Ethicists are respectful of others and do what is right when no one is looking and *even if it is hard.* And this book will show you there are a lot of *"even if"* and *"what if"* situations in life.

What if I do the right thing in reporting the fraud and lose my job in retaliation? *What if* I report a friend for plagiarism and I lose a friendship? Should I correct that financial statement error... *even if* it costs me my bonus? Or, even as extreme as, should I save that life... *even if* I risk my own?

Through it all, The Everyday Ethicist respects others and has the courage to do the right thing. The keys are simple ethical actions *(not just talk)*, respect for others *(and yourself)*, and the courage and grit to do the right thing, regardless of the consequences.

> *"The way to gain a good reputation is to endeavor to be what you desire to appear."*
> – Socrates

BEYOND EVERYDAY ETHICS

While I think *"everyday ethics"* are of utmost importance *(clearly),* there is more that we need to dive into. After all, we read about large scale, unethical conduct every day in national and local newspapers and on the Internet. It is time to think above and beyond *everyday ethics* and think and do things that are *fundamentally* right, things that represent not only lawfulness or even professional conduct, but also represent doing things right, for the right reason, the first time.

The Everyday Ethicist that I'm talking about not only has a very special set of values, but also has the courage to speak and act according to those values... the *whistleblowers* and the *tattletales* to whom this book is dedicated.

Let's face it, most of us don't really have much to learn about right and wrong. Most individuals seem to develop a keen sense of right and wrong as children. *Think about Benjamin.* But application later in life is a completely different story. So, most of this book is not going try to define right and wrong *(I believe it should be clear)* but will deal with applying what we already know as individuals, leaders, and organizations.

The content of this book is applicable for everyone, everyday; however, the book is intended for employees in workplaces, large and small; leaders in every capacity *(that make decisions and influence others),* and organizations that see the wisdom in developing an ethical culture. *So again, pretty much everyone.*

THE EVERYDAY ETHICIST: DEFINED

So, *everyone,* here is your first look at the basic "Jo-pedia" definition of The Everyday Ethicist *(more to come):*

√ They follow the basics of an ethical life – they do not lie, they do not steal, they do not cause harm to others. They keep promises. They remember the things we grew up learning.

√ They obey the letter of laws, regulations, legal requirements, and conduct guides of our societies, in spirit and intent.

√ They honor the values and codes of ethical conduct for their professions and organizations.

√ They understand that sometimes conflicts occur between ethical conduct and self-interest, and they always choose the ethical path. They understand we *always* have a *choice.*

√ They respect confidentiality and privacy of others and have a basic underlying concern for others through stewardship, trusteeship, and fiduciary principles.

√ They value character in all relationships. They are trustworthy and conscientious in determining what is right and acting upon it.

√ They stand up to defend ethical conduct whenever necessary and model ethical behavior for others.

√ They appreciate the importance of doing the right things, for the right reasons, the first time.

To sum up, The Everyday Ethicist is all about what *ought* to be done, not what *can* be done *(see Chapters Three and Four).*

The Everyday Ethical Leader *(see Chapter Five)* does what *ought* to be done, not just what *can* be done.

And The Everyday Ethical Organization *(see Chapters Seven through Ten),* full of Everyday Ethicists and Everyday Ethical Leaders, has a culture that promotes what *ought* to be done, not just what *can* be done.

Okay, I know what you are already thinking... "This doesn't seem *that* difficult"... or "I am *already* ethical." But news flash, it's not that easy. Remember the John C. Maxwell quote at the end of the preface? *"Living an ethical life may not always be easy...."*

So, it's time to learn that none of us is as ethical as we think we are. That's the Ethical Mirage.

CHAPTER TWO:

THE ETHICAL MIRAGE

(WE ARE NOT AS ETHICAL AS WE THINK WE ARE)

HAVE YOU EVER HAD an illegal download of music or other media *(TV show, movie, picture)* on your computer or phone? Statistics show that even with the rise in ease of streaming, over a third of the population still pirates music, and they just plain don't care that it's illegal.

> *"Every age group in America is less trusting than the one before... and that is for good reason:*
> *People are less trustworthy."*
> – David Brooks

Researchers planted more than 17,000 lost wallets across 355 cities in 40 countries and kept track of how many *"finders"* contacted the owner. Only 51% did. *Would you?* I know, you immediately cannot even believe I would ask you this question. But, remember 49% of people didn't.

Nearly half of workers surveyed by staffing companies say they know someone who lied on their resume. Fifty-three percent of managers have a sneaking suspicion that candidates are often dishonest, and 38% have rejected an applicant after discovering lies in the hiring process.

National surveys have reported that over 50% of graduate students across all fields of study *(e.g., business, law, engineering, education)* admit to cheating on exams. Researchers also suggest since the data is based on self-reporting, the number is probably underestimated. And studies show that test participants are more likely to cheat when paid for performance, particularly when there is no way to detect the cheating.

The *"founding father"* of research regarding academic integrity, Donald McCabe of Rutgers University, has observed that there is a generation that has an attitude of indifference to cheating. McCabe reports that students have a *"willing to do anything to get the job done"* attitude and outlook.

David Brooks in his book, *The Road to Character,* cites survey sources that indicate a decline in social trust:

"In the early 1960s, significant majorities said that people can generally be trusted. But in the 1990s the distrusters had a 20 percentage point margin over the trusters."

In Brook's book, *The Second Mountain*, he cites a study at the Harvard Graduate School of Education where middle school and high school students were asked whether they thought *"their parents cared more about personal achievements or whether they were kind."* Eighty percent said their parents cared more about achievements.

A little closer to home – if you are in my same profession – Big Four auditors *(including partners)* were complicit in using stolen regulatory data to gain a competitive advantage. And when ethics and integrity training was mandated by a regulatory agency, cheating in various forms on the *ETHICS* training was discovered.

More generally, marketers and advertisers inundate potential consumers with misleading *(at best)* information to achieve their sales goals.

Lately, many *(maybe most)* journalists have adopted a political stance and regularly tell only the part of the *"news"* story that serves their political interests. It is increasingly difficult to determine what is fake news – planted with malice and foresight by bad actors – biased news, incomplete news, manipulated news, and what is the real honest, fact-based, truth news.

Just for the record, the core ethical principles of journalism are truth and accuracy, independence, farness and impartiality, humanity *(do no harm)*, and accountability *(errors are corrected)*. How would you rate journalistic integrity in the U.S. these days? According to 2018 Gallup poll, most Americans don't trust the news media outlets *(TV and print)*. The only major institutional category surveyed that was lower in trust is the U.S. Congress. But it's not all bad news; Americans do generally trust small businesses and the military.

Sissela Bok, who is a Senior Visiting Fellow at the Harvard School of Public Health, is a well-respected American philosopher, ethicist, and author. She expressed considerable doubt about the veracity of all types of institutions in her book, *Lying: Moral Choice in Public and Private Life*, published in 1978. But her words about the prevalence of deception and declining trust could have easily been written today.

Attorneys are master manipulators of the truth on behalf of their clients – innocent or guilty *(as sin)* alike. What happened to the whole truth and nothing but the truth? Bok asks, *"Do we want a society where lawyers can implicitly promise to guard their client secrets through perjury and lies?"* When is lying for clients of all professions justified, if at all? And we wonder why the criminal justice system is one of the least trusted institutions in America.

Those running for election regularly deceive the public in order to obtain an advantage, counting on the electorate to either not care or understand. *"Much deceit for private gain masquerades as being in the public's interest,"* from Bok again. Not much has changed since she wrote those words.

"Imagine a society, no matter how ideal in other respects, where word and gesture could never be counted upon."
– Sissela Bok

HOW DO YOU RATE?

So, with all this in mind, think about how you would *honestly* rate your ethics?

I believe our personal ethics *(and in turn our overall character)* is tested daily in many ways... ways that can seem small or inconsequential, but, in reality, can have a big impact.

For instance, you're at the store and the cashier forgets to ring up a $2.00 item. *Do you say something?* Or do you let it go... thinking, *it's only a couple bucks.*

Same scenario except now your bank statement shows a $2,000 deposit and you only deposited $1,000. *Now, do you say something?*

In other words, do you put a price tag on your ethics? Or do you act with integrity at *any* cost?

> *"We are going to take things from each other if we have a chance... many people need controls around them for them to do the right thing."*
> – Dan Ariely

Dan Ariely is the James B. Duke Professor of Psychology and Behavioral Economics at Duke University. In his books *The (Honest) Truth About Dishonesty* and *Predictably Irrational*, Ariely explains *"most of us think of ourselves as honest, but, in fact, we all cheat."*

Even though most of us think of ourselves *(but not necessarily of others)* as having high moral and ethical standards, we regularly exhibit a tendency to cheat about some things, intentionally or unintentionally. Interesting *(and somewhat scary)* stuff.

SOME (UN)ETHICAL EXAMPLES

When we think of cheating in a business setting, most would likely mention Enron, the American energy, commodities, and services company based in Houston, Texas. It was founded in 1985, at its peak employed about 27,000 people, and had revenues of nearly $101 billion. Enron was named Fortune magazine's "America's Most Innovative Company" for six consecutive years. The company filed bankruptcy in 2001 and ceased to exist in 2006.

But Enron is best known for its fraud and corruption. Executives engaged in a massive accounting fraud that ultimately was uncovered. So, why all the lying?

> *"There are many motivations to commit fraud; most of them are greed related."*
> – Biegelman and Bartow

Enron's executives' instincts were not to be honest and forthright, but to see every problem or regulatory obstacle as something that could be solved by financial engineering and accounting fraud. The pressure to *"hit the number*s*"* was so great that a fictitious set of financials were created.

The Chief Financial Officer (CFO) of Enron, Andy Fastow, eventually plead guilty to accounting fraud and served five years in prison. In Eugene Soltes book, *Why They Cheat*, Fastow is quoted as saying, *"I was doing exactly what I was incentivized to do. We were finding ways to get around the rule... I cheated fair and square."* Wow. I'll leave that there for you to digest.

****

I am a part-time professor at several Denver, Colorado area colleges/universities. I teach Business, Accounting, and Auditing courses. In a recent Internal Audit class, in spite of being given explicit information about the dangers and penalties of plagiarism, one student *(who honestly completed original work, I think)* proceeded to "share" their completed project with other students.

One student who had access to the work, made very few *(if any)* changes and turned in the work as their own. When the students were questioned later, there was very obviously some lying and cover-up, so it was never quite clear just how much cheating occurred. In any event, the students *(Accounting majors)* were pretty casual about the ordeal. This scared me a bit about our future accountants and auditors.

****

I am pretty sure everyone in the world can associate the name Bernie Madoff with cheating. He became famous for running a financial Ponzi scheme – a form of fraud that lures investors and pays profits to earlier investors with funds from more recent investors. The scheme leads investors to believe that profits are generated legitimately when they are not. The scheme lasted decades and created billions in fraudulent profits. Madoff finally confessed in 2008 *(when the financial crisis blew open the scam)* and is now serving a 150 year prison sentence. So, why would a long-time respected former Wall Street executive and *"generous"* philanthropist do it?

Again, in Eugene Soltes book, *Why They Cheat*, Soltes writes that Madoff saw himself not as one who set out to intentionally create a fraud but someone who *"finds himself trapped in a business situation and makes the tragic mistake that he believes will eventually work itself out."* As Soltes states, Madoff saw himself as someone who intended to start and run a legitimate enterprise but who *"engaged in duplicity rather than see his business slow or fail."*

Madoff, as a former Chairman of the NASDAQ stock market, knew the rules of Wall Street very well, and, more importantly, per Soltes, he knew that *"legitimate and illegitimate practices blurred."* He chose to blur the lines and violate the rules, but he saw his dishonesty not so different from others in the financial services industry *(except in magnitude of the fraud).*

Madoff has shown little remorse, has an inability to relate to the chaos he caused, and is reported to have little empathy for those who lost money in his scheme.

> *"It's not like going to a bank with a gun and saying, give me your money, and running out.*
> *All I did was make rich people richer and I made some rich people poorer, but not poor."*
> – Bernie Madoff

Clearly, Madoff was not as ethical as he thought he was.

****

I heard a story recently of someone who was raised in a conservative all-American Midwestern church-going family. His father was a minister and his mother was a stay-at-home mom. He was the smartest in his class and graduated college Magna Cum Laude.

But he had a propensity to want to get an extra advantage. For example, he accumulated term papers and stole tests for himself and distributed them to his fraternity brothers. He knew he was particularly smart already, but it became a game to see if he could do even better.

Well, he grew up and succeeded spectacularly in business and was a respected leader in the community, until he was indicted by the U.S. Securities and Exchange Commission (SEC) for accounting fraud involving inflating earnings. He lost his job as a CFO and paid a big fine. That's the way he ended his career.

> *"A life directed chiefly toward fulfillment of personal desires sooner or later always leads to bitter disappointment."*
> – Albert Einstein

As a side note to this story, I taught an Ethics course for a Public Accounting firm in 2019. After taking a short ethics quiz with a *"what would you do"* question related to answers to an exam being posted on social media, the only partner in the room full of associates/managers stood up and announced his official position in his fraternity was to collect past exams to share them with everyone. When I asked him point blankly if he would do it again – looking back now – he said *"absolutely."* Just a little more food for thought. I'm sure it left an impression on those in the room, the same way it did on me.

> *"When regard for truth has been broken down or even slightly weakened, all things will remain doubtful."*
> – St. Augustine

****

CHEATING IS NOT THE MIRAGE

Academics for decades have been conducting experiments about cheating. They are detailed in numerous books, articles, and research papers. Professor Ariely has conducted many experiments and the conclusions are clear:

> *Given the opportunity, many people will cheat.*

Ariely and his team set up an experiment with students that paid a monetary reward for timed problem solving. When the students were given an opportunity to report their own results *(as opposed to evaluation of work by the instructor)*, many of the students inflated their scores.

The next experiment tested the theory of whether the probability of getting caught influenced the amount of cheating. The results showed that there was not much difference in the amount of cheating when the monitoring was varied.

> *The probability of getting caught doesn't influence many cheaters. They still cheat!*

The overall conclusion of the various Ariely *"cheating"* studies was that people may not be overly influenced by money or the threat of getting caught; however, many will cheat to obtain an advantage *"up to a level that allows us to retain our self-image as reasonably honest individuals."* Not very encouraging but definitely supports this chapter title. Individuals seem to have created their own ethical *"mirage"* self-image: *"something that appears real or possible but is not in fact so."*

TURN YOUR AWARENESS UP

So, why are we not as ethical as we think we are? There's clearly a lot of reasons. It's this apparent human tendency for everyone to cheat a little. It's our human nature to rationalize away poor behavior *(and we get really creative at it at times – see Chapter Four, The Ethical Rationalizer)*. It's a whole bunch of conflicts of interest coming from all directions. It's a gradual shift, one unethical act often leads to another... and another. It's emulating the poor behavior of others *(perhaps even our leaders – think about my story about the partner at the public accounting firm)* and a culture, in general, which venerates poor role models.

But the good news *(if you can call it that),* as Ariely states is:

> *"Recognizing our shortcomings is the crucial first step on the path to making better decisions, creating better societies, and fixing our institutions."*

So, let's start here. It's time to understand we are not as ethical as we think we are, recognize our shortcomings, and get to work on our decisions, institutions, and society, in general.

THIS IS THE ETHICAL MIRAGE PROPOSITION.

The next step on the path to Becoming The Everyday Ethicist is to develop your personal strategy to act ethically in all situations. And, I believe that begins by establishing and focusing on Ethical Anchors.

EXPLORE YOUR ETHICAL MIRAGE

How might poor character and integrity limit your personal and professional life?

Do you believe a person can be ethical and still succeed?

Do you believe a person can be unethical and still succeed?

Do you think it is possible to use one set of ethical standards for all areas of your life?

Can you recall someone who has made poor ethical choices? How did that work out for them? What was the impact?

What are the characteristics of someone that you cannot trust? Describe and explain.

Describe conflicts of interest present in your life and how you handle them.

How do you respond to pressure?

What are the factors that most often derail your ethics? What are your weaknesses?

Do you admit ethical mistakes and change course to improve?

How do you or can you guard against ethical lapses?

CHAPTER THREE:

ETHICAL ANCHORS

(FOR OUR CONDUCT)

ON TO ETHICAL ANCHORS, the cornerstones of becoming The Everyday Ethicist, being an ethical leader, and creating an ethical organization culture.

What would a book about ethics be without reference to the cornerstones *(anchors)* of philosophical thought and philosophers from the past? Let's review the primary schools of thought about ethics and morality. We will use Benjamin's experience with the squirrel to keep it simple *(and perhaps more fun)* and help explain. *(Plus, I get to brag on my son a little and show his picture again. Bonus mom points.)*

We learned in Chapter One that Benjamin *"caught the squirrel"* and we explored what Benjamin and Aristotle had in common. He instinctively thought that catching the squirrel was the *"right"* thing to do. But let's explore some other ethics philosophies and see other reasons he may have wanted to catch that squirrel....

BENJAMIN THE UTILITARIAN

If Benjamin had been a utilitarian philosopher, he would have been thinking about catching the squirrel to do the greatest good for the greatest number of people. He would have been thinking like Jeremy Bentham (1748 – 1832), an English moral philosopher, who founded the doctrine of utilitarianism. So, if my son had been born in the 18th or 19th century, he may have regularly caught squirrels and ran home to his mother with a welcome contribution for dinner *("oh boy," says his mom)*. In Benjamin's small circle with no laws or regulations to complicate matters about squirrel catching, that's as utilitarian as it gets. The family was happy.

An extreme case of utilitarianism plays out in the true story of the Essex whaler described in the Nathaniel Philbrick non-fiction history of the episode, *In the Heart of the Sea.*

The Essex was launched in 1799. It went on its final voyage in 1819. While at sea in the Pacific, it was attacked and sunk by a sperm whale. Stranded thousands of miles from land with little food and water, the 20-man crew made for land in the surviving whaleboats. With severe dehydration, starvation, and exposure on the open ocean, the survivors eventually resorted to eating the bodies of the crewmen who had died. When that proved insufficient, members of the crew drew lots to determine whom they would sacrifice so the others could live.

That's utilitarianism – the greatest good for the greatest number of people. But, was it ethical and morally defensible?

> *"Ethics is knowing the difference between what you have a right to do and what is right to do."*
> – Potter Stewart

BENJAMIN THE LIBERTARIAN

On with Benjamin and the squirrel. If Benjamin was a libertarian, he would follow the teachings of John Locke (1632-1704), the English philosopher known as "The Father of Liberalism." Benjamin might decide to keep the squirrel for himself *(over the objections of his mother)* claiming his rights trumped the rights of any others. He would do what he pleased with the squirrel since he caught it. And taking the squirrel away from him would be fundamentally unfair and unethical.

Or, Benjamin the libertarian could have changed his mind altogether and said, "I'M NOT CATCHING THE SQUIRREL!" The squirrel is free to do what it wants including jumping out of trees and falling to its injury or death. He is not going to interfere as long as no one is throwing the squirrel out of the tree. Libertarians respect the rights of others *(even squirrels)* as long as they do not interfere with their own rights.

BENJAMIN THE KANTIAN

If my son were a Kantian, he would show more empathy for the fate of the squirrel *(and certainly would be empathetic to the fate of the sailors on the Essex)*. Immanuel Kant (1724 – 1804) offered an alternative to utilitarianism or libertarianism. He believed in and respected the fundamental rights of others *(yes, even squirrels again)* to live. A Kantian might give the squirrel to the humane society or risk death before resorting to eating it.

Immanuel Kant believed that each human being deserved dignity and respect, regardless of circumstance. He believed in doing the right thing because it was right, not for any ulterior motive. Benjamin the Kantian would give no thought to any praise he might get for saving the squirrel or the damage that might be done to himself as a result of catching the squirrel *(they may be cute, but they bite, remember)*.

BENJAMIN THE SOCIAL CONTRACT THEORIST

If Benjamin was a follower of John Rawls (1921 – 2002), an American moral and political philosopher, he would consider what his buddies wanted to do with the squirrel after he caught it *(or they would have all decided together whether to even catch it in the first place)*.

Collectively, what do we think is fair and just? Do we have it for dinner? Do we keep it as a pet? Do we let it go? Rawls would ask all of society to make a rational decision, all things considered. Benjamin would set aside his own convictions and accept the decision made by the group – a social contract. It's really group think in action *(more to come in Chapter Four on group think)*.

> *"The hard part of intellectual life is separating what is true from what will get you liked."*
> – David Brooks

WHICH THEORY DO WE CHOOSE?

So, which theory is the best *"anchor"* for ethical decision making? Is utilitarian the best – the greatest good for the greatest number? Is libertarianism the best – what is good for me is good for all? Is Kantism the best – respect for each and every person's rights? Or is social contract theory best – let the group decide what's right? Each of these could be elaborated much further, but I hope this gave you a good summary. And I am hoping the squirrel brought some level of entertainment.

I am guessing by now you can probably think of pitfalls of each ethical approach. None, by itself, blends the qualities of welfare and utility, freedom, respect for others, as well as the social good. But Benjamin, the shipwrecked sailors, you, and I have to make decisions. So, what do we do?

BACK TO BENJAMIN THE LITTLE ARISTOTLE

Fortunately, we still have Aristotle's Nicomachean Ethics (384 – 322 B.C.) and theory of justice. It is doing the right thing, *"to the right person, to the right extent, at the right time, with the right motive, and in the right way."* Now that takes a lot of thought – to identify the highest human good under the circumstances. Aristotle suggests that people who are good citizens can do just and proper things through deliberation of the common good, weighing the alternatives, arguing various positions, and making fair and reasonable decisions, all things considered.

> *"Treat people as if they were what they ought to be and you will help them become what they are capable of becoming."*
> – Johann Wolfgang von Goethe

****

I have set the past philosophical *"stage"* for making ethical decisions. And I do think there was a little here and there that should help us all. But now I am going to introduce my favorite *"actors"* from a cross section of today's greatest teachers, leaders, and thinkers, all of whom are concerned with ethics.

As helpful as the lessons from the past philosophers may be, I believe simpler, more pragmatic lessons may be even more helpful to anchor ourselves in ethical decision making, ethical leadership, and establishing ethical organizations.

> *"Chase after the truth like all hell and you'll free yourself, even though you (may) never touch its coat tails."*
> – Clarence Darrow

Let's start our chase for more ethical anchors with...

THE ETHICS CHECK

(Note: Unless otherwise noted, quotes in this section are by Kenneth Blanchard and Norman Vincent Peale.)

In their book, *The Power of Ethical Management,* Kenneth Blanchard and Norman Vincent Peale present a way to *"ethically anchor yourself"* (my words, not theirs) based on a combination of law, corporate/organizational values, and personal conscience questions:

1. *Is it legal?* Will the decisions or actions violate either civil law or organization policy?

2. *Is it balanced?* Are the decisions or actions fair to all concerned in the short-term as well as the long-term? And, do the decisions or actions promote win-win relationships for all stakeholders?

3. *How will the decisions or actions make me feel about myself?* Will the decisions or actions make me proud of

myself? Would I feel good about myself if the decisions or actions were described publicly? How would my family feel about me when they became aware?

Blanchard and Peale believe that asking the three simple questions in difficult situations can guide all into a *"pattern of right behavior that will become habit-forming."*

In their book, they describe a hypothetical situation of a sales manager pressured to hire someone on the basis that the individual will provide confidential information from a competitor. The tug is between the potential positive impact on sales from the valuable information, pressure from senior management *(who simply want results any way possible)* with the knowledge of the illegality of the action, and the guilty conscience and vulnerability of the hiring manager. Unfortunately, life is full of these conflicting situations, but the conclusion offered in the book is:

> *"If we have to cheat to win, then we better think twice about what we are doing."*

It is usually not difficult *(following the three questions)* to know what is *"right"* but deciding to make the *"right"* decisions and take the *"right"* action can be difficult.

> *"Being an ethical person means behaving ethically all the time – not only when it is convenient.*
> *In fact, it is especially important to act ethically when it is inconvenient or unpopular to do so."*

Is it time to "check your ethics?"

****

THE GOLDEN RULE

(Note: Unless otherwise noted, quotes in this section are by John C. Maxwell.)

John C. Maxwell, leadership expert, speaker, pastor, and author of 22 books *(New York Times best sellers, sold millions)* wrote a pretty simple little book titled, *There's No Such thing As "Business" Ethics.* Seem like a strange title for a business ethics book? I thought so. But after reading a bit I got the message:

> *"... a single standard applies to both your business and personal life – and it's one we all know and trust. The Golden Rule."*

When I started looking for practical, down-to-earth *"ethical anchors,"* Maxwell's argument for the *"Golden Rule"* hit the mark. We are all familiar with the Golden Rule *(treat others as you want to be treated)* in our lives, but Maxwell makes a strong case for the Golden Rule application to business.

Maxwell first describes what he calls the Ethical Dilemma – situations where we are tempted to do what is self-serving and convenient, rather than ethical. He also describes situations typical of business where the drive to win is so compelling that we compromise our ethical standards. We practice situational ethics and rationalize questionable ethical conduct.

Maxwell then describes various options to instill higher standards of ethics, such as teaching remedial ethics in schools and organizations, harsh treatment of offenders, and relying on the legal standards. But Maxwell believes none of the above is sufficient.

Finally, Maxwell asks the question,

> *What could be a universal guide for ethical decision making?*

... where you would *always* be considered as making the ethical choice?

You guessed it. Follow the Golden Rule. Ask the question *"How would I like to be treated in this situation?"* If this was the principle guide to decision making, would the result be impeccable integrity? Maxwell thinks so and so do I.

Why? Well, because as Maxwell points out, a version of the Golden Rule exists in every culture. It's easy to understand. It's a win-win approach – who is unhappy when you treat people like you would like to be treated? And the Golden Rule standard never changes, even as circumstances do.

> *"The Golden Rule is good for employees. It's good for clients. And it's good for investors."*

Decisions, not conditions or circumstances, determine your ethics. No matter how much pressure from others, stay the Golden Rule ethical course. Become predictably trustworthy.

Don't succumb to the lure of pleasures, become drunk with power, or develop an exaggerated sense of worth. Do set priorities with honesty, integrity, and character at the top. Take responsibility for your actions, develop personal discipline, know your weaknesses, and place high value in your family and associates. All good advice from Maxwell.

> *"Make your decisions based on the Golden Rule guideline."*
>
> Start by *"treating people better than they treat you."*
>
> *"Giving truly is the highest level of living. It makes the world a better place."*
>
> *"You can go for the gold or go for the Golden Rule."*

ETHICAL LESSONS WE LEARNED AS CHILDREN

(Note: Unless otherwise noted, quotes in this section are by Jon M. Huntsman.)

The late Jon M. Huntsman (1937 – 2018) was an American businessman and philanthropist. He was the founder and CEO of Huntsman Corporation, a former Navy officer, and received numerous awards for his leadership. As a humanitarian, it has been reported that Huntsman gave away over $1.5 billion in his lifetime. And, he felt so strongly about ethical conduct that he wrote a book about it titled *Winners Never Cheat: Everyday Values We Learned as Children (But May Have Forgotten).* Long title but a very straightforward, simple message.

(Note: Huntsman later updated the book (post 2008 recession) to deal with ethical issues "Even in Difficult Times." Same basic message, different circumstances.)

Huntsman explains that he grew up under modest circumstances in rural Idaho. He says he was taught to be tough, be competitive, but to play by the rules. Play fairly. He says he developed a value system learned in homes, sandboxes, playgrounds, classrooms, Sunday schools, and athletic fields that took him to the leadership of a world class business and to an honorable and satisfying personal life. Must have been a pretty good value system. It starts with...

> *"Be fair, don't cheat, play nicely, share and share alike, tell the truth."*

Huntsman truly believed that childhood prescriptions can *(and did in his case)* lead to success in all fields and *"more happiness in home and work."*

Huntsman tells the story of when he was a young man working in the Nixon White House as a staff secretary. It was Watergate time and, to make a long story short, he was asked by a senior member of Nixon's team to do something that he believed was unethical *(to support Nixon's political goals)*. As Huntsman describes, *"it took me about 15 minutes for my inner moral compass to make itself noticed,"* and he proceeded to tell the second most powerful man in America that he wasn't going to do it. And, shortly thereafter, he left the job in the White House. Moral to the story is,

> *"Grey does not substitute for black and white."*

Huntsman points out that, throughout the world, every decent human being values honesty over deceit. But he also points out that we live in a world where it seems to be popular to look for an unfair advantage – to cheat a little. In today's society, winners are those who deceive others without getting caught. But Huntsman believes that we all know when we are *"approaching the boundary"* and *"don't feel quite right."* It is back to basics of childhood lessons.

> *"We know darn well what is right and wrong."*

More childhood basics: Do what you're supposed to do when you are told to do it. Never tell lies. Cover your mouth when you cough or sneeze *(timeless advice, but especially important in 2020; thank you for the additional reminder, COVID-19)*. Call out liars and cheaters. Don't cut in line. Express gratitude and praise, without prompt. Keep your word and don't be rude. Good sportsmanship and table manners count. When you see someone in trouble, reach out to them.

Don't be pressured into unethical conduct because *"everyone does it"* and don't offer the excuse that it is the only way to keep up – when you know that your motivation is *"arrogance, power trips, greed, and lack of backbone."* Huntsman gets right to the point... with his lessons *(or as I would call them, anchors)*:

⇒ *"Circumstances may change but your values shouldn't."*

⇒ *"Financial ends never justify unethical means."*

⇒ *"Which rules we honor and which we ignore determine personal character."*

⇒ *"Trust is a greater compliment than affection."*

⇒ *"With integrity comes respect."*

⇒ *"Say what you mean and mean what you say; don't play games."*

⇒ *"Surround yourself with associates with the courage to say no."*

⇒ *"Stand for what is right, not what is popular."*

⇒ *"Winning with class is not a definition at odds with itself."*

⇒ *"True giving is doing something for somebody who can never repay you."*

⇒ And, finally, *"win the old-fashioned way: talent, hard work, trust, fairness and honesty."*

And remember to also "anchor yourself" in the childhood lessons – they never vary.

****

ENOUGH

(Note: Unless otherwise noted, quotes in this section are by John C. Bogle.)

John C. Bogle (1929-2019) is, to me, the model for character, ethics, and integrity. Bogle was the founder of The Vanguard Group of mutual funds. He served as the chief executive of Vanguard from its founding in 1974 until 1999.

Bogle was often referred to as the *"conscience of Wall Street"* – a position he held all by himself! He was the creator of the first index fund, championed low-cost investing, and was a disruptor *(in a good, ethical way)* of the mutual fund industry. He received significant praise and recognition from many, but specifically by Warren Buffet who stated, *"John Bogle has done more for the individual investor than anyone else in history."* And I say, Bogle did it in an honorable way.

He wrote twelve books throughout his life, all with a theme of character, stewardship, corporate values, customer focus, and community service. He died in 2019 and left behind enormous insight and advice.

In his book, *Enough: True Measures of Money, Business, and Life*, written in 2009, Bogle provides a framework for ethics in business and life. To Bogle, an ethical life and business is about creating a proper balance, and he definitely felt that ethics has gotten out of balance over the years.

Bogle believed the ethics imbalance has been a detriment to individuals, leaders, organizations, and society in general. The general theme of his *"Enough"* book is about excesses in all forms. He described areas where there is *"too much"* or *"not enough."*

So, how do you restore the proper balance? Bogle had some suggestions, many of which had to do with character and integrity. All serve as good *"ethical anchors."*

Too Much Success, Not Enough Character

Bogle believed that society places *"too much"* importance on the traditional measures of success of fame, power, and wealth. And, he believed that financial wealth in particular is *"a shallow measure of success."* Bogle asks, fame and power are ego builders, but what are they really worth?

Bogle observes that millions of people *(without wealth, power, and fame)* have had *"an enormous and positive impact on their communities."* Think of those for whom you have great respect for their community impact. Is the source of their impact fame, power, and wealth? Most likely not. At the same time, reflect on those with great wealth, power, and fame that have caused great damage. These are Bogle's observations and questions.

His conclusion: Success should not be measured in monetary terms, by the amount of power one has over others, or by the *"illusory fame of . . . transitory public notice."* According to Bogle, an ethical individual, leader, or organization measures success in what is contributed to society. And *"no success is the right success if it is achieved at society's expense."*

My all-time, simple, yet favorite Bogle quote:

"What does it all mean if you lack honor and character?"

After a career in the financial services industry, Bogle became a critic of the industry based on *"too much cost"* and *"not enough value"* to customer/investors. What is good for the financial services industry is often bad for its customers.

Bogle elaborates on many other *"too much"* and *"not enough"* situations and mindsets, most of which relate to ethical conduct. For instance, there is *"too much complexity"* when it's used to cover-up, confuse, and obfuscate and results in *"not enough truth."*

Bogle describes the many business transactions that are driven by *"too much counting"* (i.e., financial shenanigans) and *"not enough trust."* Bogle hoped for and encouraged all to engage in a more *"enlightened sense of human values and ethical standards"* for all interactions with stakeholders and associates.

"Not everything that counts can be counted, and not everything that can be counted counts."

Bogle saw a world driven more and more by *"too much business conduct"* with an anything goes mentality and *"not enough professional conduct,"* which generally operates under ethics and integrity standards first and foremost.

"... we can demand that a business conduct its affairs with ethical professionalism."

There is *"not enough"* space in this book and *"too much"* to be covered. Read Bogle's book and grab more of Bogle's ethical anchors and pull them into your soul.

And follow the Bogle Rule: Make "caring" your number one ethical value.

****

THE ROAD TO CHARACTER

(Note: Unless otherwise noted, quotes in this section are by David Brooks.)

David Brooks, author, New York Times columnist, and PBS commentator, wrote *The Road to Character* in 2015. It was received with much acclaim and has become a staple of mine when I speak about ethics issues. There will be more about Brook's concepts in Chapter Four; however, I believe one of Brook's themes in particular deserves consideration for becoming an *"ethical anchor."*

Like Bogle, Brooks sees deterioration in ethical standards in today's society and has data and observation to back it up. In effect, there is not enough ethical anchors and ethical behavior. He writes about the deterioration in the balance *(there's that balance concept again)* between external accomplishments and our internal moral and ethical lives. Brooks talks to us about virtues and vices and the struggle between them and the need to become more self-aware as we build and develop our character traits.

Brooks sees a modern culture that has lost its way in teaching a new generation the path to building character. He observes people are *"more isolated, more self-absorbed, and less able to engage in moral reasoning."*

Admittedly, Brooks does a lot of preaching, but it is good, meaningful, impactful preaching:

"We all have a moral responsibility to be moral every day."

"Be better than you used to be, be dependable in times of testing, and straight in times of temptation."

So, what is Brook's ethical anchor? It is understanding the difference between *"resume virtues"* and *"eulogy virtues."*

Resume virtues are *(obviously)* the ones that you list on your resume – skills that you bring to the job market that contribute to external success *(remember – wealth, power, and fame)*.

Eulogy virtues are the ones that get talked about at your funeral; the ones that exist at the *"core of your being."* They relate to whether you are kind, courageous, and honest. They relate to the types of relationships you form throughout your life.

Brooks believes that society today encourages *"resume virtues"* and the competition to succeed, satisfy our desires, have fast and shallow communication, and *"turn everything into a game."* And, in the process, we lose sight of moral and ethical stakes.

"If you don't have some inner integrity, eventually your Watergate, your scandal, your betrayal, will happen."

The resume approach wins victories over others; the eulogy approach wins victories over ethical weaknesses.

"Build character by winning victories over weaknesses."

Brooks asks all the right questions. What are your personal and professional character standards? Do you minimize ethical issues? Do you think of ethical choices clearly, or blindly? Do you make small compromises that later become larger issues?

Brooks reminds us through his profiles of people *(that include Dorothy Day, George Marshall, Francis Perkins, Dwight Eisenhower and more)* from different times and mostly, periods of adversity. They all had firm ethical anchors that served them well at critical times.

"... the tales of the excellent can lift the ambitions of the living."

Through the examples, Brooks reminds us that *The Road to Character* is built by moderation and thoughtful decision making, taking a stand when necessary, speaking the truth even at personal risk, being ethically and morally dependable, and *"avoiding the impulse to live for today... plundering... tomorrow."*

"Be passionate about the ends but deliberate about the proper means to realize them."

True character fulfillment comes not from *"realization of the wants"* but *"moral traditions"* and *"obligations to community and country."* Brooks summed things up pretty well by saying,

"To lead a better life you just have to work harder, or use more will power, or make better decisions...
play by the rules, take care of things yourself... be the cause of your own good life."

And, if you want to continue your character growth from the "here and now" to the future, read Brook's book, *The Second Mountain.*

And definitely follow "The Road to Character" along the way.

****

LYING, HAPPINESS, AND ETHICS

(Note: Unless otherwise noted, quotes in this section are by Sissela Bok.)

Now, there's an interesting combination – lying, happiness, and ethics. *Right?*

Sissela Bok is considered one of the premier American moral philosophers. She is a former college professor of philosophy and is currently a Senior Visiting Fellow at the Harvard School of Public Health. Her book, *Lying: Moral Choice in Public and Private Life*, has been described as one of the most significant philosophy books in the 20th century. Bok has written about some of the greatest moral issues of our time including those related to medical advances, death and dying, higher education, war, and the law.

First, let's explore Bok's position on lying. She recognizes that under limited circumstances, a little white lie may be appropriate to preserve relationships. *Honey, you look really thin in that dress. Or, dear, I like it that you are balding prematurely. (And yes, perhaps these are things my husband and I say to each other...)* She says, *"They preserve the equilibrium and often the humaneness of social relationships."*

But more importantly on the subject of lying, Bok recognizes *"the very stress on individualism, on competition, on achieving material success... generates intense pressure to cut corners."* She recognizes *"the social incentives to deceive at present are very powerful; the controls often weak."*

"It is easy... to tell a lie, but hard to tell only one."

Bok feels a real problem coming when lying is considered normal. She asks and answers her own question, *"Must we take levels of deception to be our lot? There is no reason to think so."*

Bok takes on serious issues about lying. She questions the ethics of government officials who deceive *"when they think they can get away with it."* She questions lawyers who *"manipulate the truth in court on behalf of their clients."* She questions those in selling, advertising, or any form of advocacy *"that may mislead the public and their competitors in order to achieve their goals."* And she questions journalists, law enforcement, and intelligence officials who *"have little compunction in using falsehoods to gain the knowledge they seek."*

She believes organizations must take on more responsibility for changing the pressures and incentives to lie. She is an absolute advocate of codes of ethics and states, *"methods of disciplining those who infringe the guidelines must be given teeth and enforced."* She also believes that educational institutions have a *"large role to play"* in setting professional standards, setting expectations for upholding the standards, and preparing students for dealing with duplicity when and where encountered.

Bok reminds us that...

> *"Trust and integrity are precious resources, easily squandered, hard to regain.*
> *They thrive only on a foundation of respect for veracity."*

Bok' latest book, *Exploring Happiness: From Aristotle to Brain Science*, explores the connections between ethics and happiness. It turns out there are a lot of connections.

And since I believe there is generally a common desire to be happy *and* ethical, I went on the search for another anchor. Here is what I found.

Bok has reflected on the connection between what makes us happy *(an individual pursuit)* and ethics and morality *(i.e., the way we treat others).* She explores the dangers of spending too much time focused on self-interest *(to make ourselves happy)* and the potential conflicts that turn into unethical pursuits.

Bernie Madoff – How happy were you, really?

Happiness may be defined subjectively or scientifically. There may be differences in how happiness is defined or what constitutes happiness, how it is attained and sustained. However, there should be no dispute that happiness should not come at the expense of others.

Happiness should not be exclusively based on how we lead our lives; it should be focused on the happiness of others *(how we treat others)* as well. This is the ethical part. If happiness were to be only focused internally, there would be plenty of room for happy jerks who make others' lives miserable.

"To be happy is one thing and to be good is another."

And as we know, sometimes they conflict. The answer enters the realm of ethics:

"Happiness is that state of consciousness which proceeds from the achievement of one's values."

So, here's my ethical anchor from Bok. Lying is unethical under most circumstances and happiness should never come at the expense of others.

Let's anchor ourselves in being happy AND ethical.

****

JUSTICE

(Note: Unless otherwise noted, quotes in this section are by Michael J. Sandel.)

Michael J. Sandel asks us, *what's the right thing to do?*

Sandel is a Professor of Government Theory at Harvard University and author of the book, *Justice.* He is described as one of this generation's most important philosophers. Sandel goes to great lengths to explain the various schools of thought involving ethics *(the philosophies we discussed at the beginning of this chapter)* but expresses his *"favor"* for the Aristotle approach to making decisions for *"common good"* and the *"good life."* *(I think Sandel and Benjamin would get along.)*

Sandel points out the pitfalls of utilitarianism saying that ethics should be about principles, not calculations or measure of value and cost. He cited the Ford Pinto disaster. When Ford found out in the 1970s that the Ford Pinto fuel tank was prone to explode when hit from the rear, a cost-benefit analysis was conducted and it was determined *"the benefits of fixing it (in lives saved and injuries prevented) were not worth the eleven dollars per car it would have cost to equip each car with a device that would have made the gas tank safer."*

Sandel also cited the example of the utilitarian mentality of one particular tobacco company. The company prepared a cost/benefit analysis for the Czech Republic government showing that smoking had a positive impact on the national budget; more smoking causes more premature deaths which lowers public assistance for the elderly. Wow.

Likewise, Sandel respects libertarianism's arguments of taking individual rights seriously, but he sees pitfalls in accepting *"people's preferences as they are"* without consideration on the impact on society. Is ethics only about being able

"... to do whatever we want with the things we own, provided we respect other people's rights to do the same?"

What about seatbelt laws, motorcycle helmet laws, minimum wage laws, anti-trust laws and regulations, laws regarding selling vape products to minors, and laws supporting subsidized housing or healthcare? Are the laws ethical or not – a true libertarian might ask.

Sandel mentions the price gouging of storm victims during Hurricane Charley. I'll add the hoarding and price gouging we all witnessed during the 2020 coronavirus outbreak.

Just because you can, doesn't mean you should.
(Not sure who said this first, but I say it all the time.)

Then there is Kantism, which says that every person is worthy of respect and people have a duty to do the right things for the right reasons. And, morality is about principle, not consequences – let the consequences be what they may. We have the duty to tell the truth regardless of consequences.

But Sandel says, *"Imagine yourself in a predicament with a friend hiding in a closet and a murderer at the door."* Do you lie to allow the friend to escape? Is it ethical to lie under the circumstances?

Would it be ethical for an auditor to make a request for records under false pretenses when there is a belief that the request would have been denied, had the truth been told? Think Enron. Think Madoff. So much to think about in regard to ethical principles and actions.

Justice and ethics are about reasoning and making judgments about what is good and the right thing to do.

> *"A just society requires a strong sense of community."*
>
> *"To achieve a just society, we have to reason together about the meaning of a good life...."*

Sandel ends the book by defining processes for the common good. I believe they could apply to all sizes and forms of institutions and organizations, and free societies in general.

o Constantly pursue a sense of mutual values and shared responsibility.

o Apply free market thinking, recognizing that markets may not be entirely the best way to determine social values and non-market norms.

o Continue the never-ending quest for *"distributive justice"* and the common good.

o Engage in a *"robust public engagement... to provide a basis for mutual respect."*

But Sandel also goes on to say, *"Justice is inescapably judgmental,"* which I believe is why we need these ethical anchors in the first place.

Seek justice, even if...

****

I hope after all these stages and players, you are able to choose some meaningful, thought provoking *"ethical anchors."* Study, reflect, and develop your own personal ethical anchors that will serve the life you live, the work that you do, the decisions that you make, and the organizations of which you are a part.

I close this chapter with a quick recap of the ethical anchors that have served me well:

Take the Ethics Check.

Go for The Golden Rule.

Remember Childhood Lessons.

Choose Caring; It's Enough.

Build Your Road to Character.

Be Happy *and* Ethical

And, Seek Justice, Even If.

*"Ethics is not a description of what people do;
It's a prescription for what we all should do."*
– Michael Josephson

Everyone needs to prescribe to "ethical anchors" like these.

THIS IS THE ETHICAL ANCHOR PROPOSITION.

Note: I have included a list of reference books at the end of this chapter to help you further research and find your *ethical anchors*.

Now, let's go on down the path to Becoming The Everyday Ethicist by understanding our other ethical choices: the "Big Me" and the "Ethical Rationalizer" mentalities.

EXPLORE YOUR ETHICAL ANCHORS

What are your ethical boundaries? When have you approached these boundaries personally or professionally?

What are the benefits of having ethical anchors like the ones discussed in this chapter?

What values do you believe have contributed to your successes?

What values (ignored) contributed to your adversity?

What are your ethical anchors that define your life?

How have you developed your ethical anchors throughout your life? Describe the evolution.

What professional or organizational standards exist that help define your ethical anchors?

Do you have different ethical standards for your personal life and work life? How do they differ?

Name and describe one or more persons who have been ethical anchors in your life. How have they impacted you?

ETHICAL ANCHOR REFERENCE MATERIAL

Aristotle, translated by W. D. Ross, (1908), *Nicomachean Ethics*. Pantianos Classics.

Beauchamp, Tom L., & Childress, James F. (2001). *Principles of Biomedical Ethics*. New York, NY. Oxford University Press.

Bogle, John C. (2009). *Enough*. Hoboken, NJ. John Wiley & Sons, Inc.

Bok, Sissela. (1978). *Lying: Moral Choice in Public and Private Life*. New York, NY. Patheon Books.

Bok, Sissela. (2010). *Exploring Happiness*. New Haven, CT. Yale University Press.

Brooks, David. (2015). *The Road to Character*. New York, NY. Random House.

Brooks, David. (2019). *The Second Mountain: The Quest for a Moral Life*. New York, NY. Random House.

Huntsman, Jon M. (2005). *Winners Never Cheat: Everyday Values We Learn as Children (But May Have Forgotten)*. Upper Saddle River, NJ. Wharton School Publishing.

Maxwell, John C (2003). *There's No Such Thing as "Business" Ethics*. New York, NY. Hachette Book Group.

Messick, D. M. & Tenbrunsel, A. E. (1996). *Codes of Conduct* New York, NY. Russel Sage Foundation.

Sandel, Michael J. (2009). *Justice*. New York, NY. Farrar, Straus, and Giroux.

CHAPTER FOUR:

ETHICAL CHOICES

(THE BIG ME, THE ETHICAL RATIONALIZER, AND THE EVERYDAY ETHICIST)

SO, IF WE HAVE ALL these ethical anchors influencing our lives, why does unethical conduct still sometimes seep in? Because the road isn't always an easy, straight path. We still have a choice to make to fully turn the right, ethical way.

And, the fact is, some people just seem to be oblivious to right and wrong, as Professor McCabe observed. Some people place relationships above character. Some people place their job above their character. Some cannot handle conflict of any sort nor the difficult choices thrown at us over a lifetime. Some simply rationalize away any personal responsibility in unethical conduct. But some are motivated by greed, personal glory, and power. And these *"some"* shall now be called a *"Big Me."*

THE FIRST ETHICAL CHOICE:

THE BIG ME

> *"A man wrapped up in himself makes a very small bundle."*
> – Benjamin Franklin

You have already gotten to know David Brooks through earlier discussions of his book, *The Road to Character*. Well, in the book, Brooks formally introduces the concept of the Big Me. To simplify, Brooks sees an ongoing sociological shift from a society that emphasized the integrity and trust of the individual to a society of individuals who are much more selfish, materialistic, and narcissistic. Brooks refers to current times *(2015 when the book was written)* as *"The Age of the Selfies."*

Brooks offers two data points in support of his thesis. First, he cites surveys gauging narcissism. Between 1948 and 1954, psychologists asked more than 10,000 adolescents whether they considered themselves *"to be a very important person."* The result, 12% answered "yes". In 1989, the same question was revisited and 80% of boys and 77% of girls answered "yes." Don't get me wrong, I am all for developing confidence in a child, but I'm not for developing a self-serving Big Me.

Second, he cites researchers from UCLA who conducted a national survey of college freshman *"to gauge their values and what they want out of life."* In 1966, 80% of freshman said that they were strongly motivated to develop a meaningful philosophy of life. In 2015 when Brooks wrote his book, the number *"was cut in half."* The surveys cited indicate that the primary focus had shifted over the years to money, not values.

The top American scandals in the last several decades provide supporting evidence. To me, the college admissions scandal *(uncovered in 2019)* is the classic example. There is really no other explanation than the desire to perpetuate the Big Me of those who bribed for their future Big Me's benefit.

Then, looking back in time, there were *"the smartest guys in the room"* who committed fraud and bankrupted Enron along with *the smartest auditors in the room* who were self-serving and ruined Arthur Anderson. All for power, prestige, and personal gain.

There was Dennis Kozlowski, the CEO at Tyco International and his extravagant lifestyle *(all charged to the company, of course),* until he went to jail for fraud. Call it a power trip gone wrong. As Eugene Soltes explains in his book, *Why They Do It, "executives, like other individuals in position of power, can neglect to take into account or imagine the sentiments of those around them."* And as Soltes quotes Kozlowski, *"... you become consumed a little bit by your own arrogance and you really think you can do anything."* I would say he became a lot consumed by arrogance, not a little.

There were executives at Volkswagen (VW) who perpetrated a huge emissions scandal all for the power and prestige of achieving global market share leadership.

There was the negligence and willful poor safety conduct at British Petroleum (BP) that led to the largest environmental disaster in history, all for greater profits.

The list continues – the recklessness of executives at Lehman Brothers that contributed to the 2008 financial crisis; the greed of branch employees at all levels at Wells Fargo to earn incentives by fraudulently opening customer accounts; and let's not forget the disastrous collision of Bernie Madoff's poor personal character and a Wall Street environment where *"legitimate and illegitimate practices blurred."* *(Thank you, again, Eugene Soltes.)*

As Soltes writes in his book, *"Madoff's fraud was far too large to be viewed as an isolated error in judgment. Time and time again, Madoff had the opportunity to avoid fraudulent activity..."* So, what exactly was Madoff thinking?

Madoff recounted, *"It wasn't like I was being blackmailed; it wasn't as if I couldn't have said no; I know the rules."* So, all I can surmise is with all the Wall Street fame, the philanthropy prestige, the Palm Beach home in a community of *"movers and shakers,"* Madoff was simply caught up in being the ultimate Big Me.

> *"The temptation and power – without ethics and character – make a recipe for disaster."*
> – Biegelman & Bartow

Accounting scandals of overstating earnings, cases of financial engineering, falsification of financial statements, under-reporting costs, and just plain making up numbers – mostly to fuel stock prices and pump up personal bonuses – is the Big Me in action in corporate America.

From the 49% that did not return the wallet to the 50% that cheated on graduate school exams, to the individuals and executives at the aforementioned organizations, there is a whole lot of Big Me mentality going around out there.

We've previously touched on Brook's overall message that *"people are more isolated, less likely to have empathy for others, and in general, less oriented to things like community."*

People today *"lack the ability to articulate and engage in moral reasoning...."* Just. Plain. Scary.

As John C. Bogle has stated, *"it's amazing how difficult it is for a man to understand something if he's paid a small fortune not to understand it."* This comment applies particularly well for some of the Big Me characters mentioned above. *Don't you agree?*

The bottom line: Don't be a Big Me. Don't work for a Big Me organization or boss, and don't even associate with a Big Me. It often leads to ethical trouble.

> *"It is much easier to avoid temptation altogether than to overcome it...."*
> – Dan Ariely

Quit your job before you quit your ethics. I did once.

And it was, hands down, the best decision I ever made.

****

THE SECOND ETHICAL CHOICE:

THE ETHICAL RATIONALIZER

It's OK, Son, Everyone Does It

(Variation on original by Jack Griffin)

When Johnny was 6 years old, he was with his father when they were caught speeding. His father handed the officer a $20 bill with his driver's license. *"It's OK, son,"* his father said as they drove off. *"Everybody does it."*

When he was 8, he was present at a family council presided over by Uncle George, on the surest means to shave points off the income tax return. *"It's OK, kid,"* his uncle said. *"Everybody does it."*

When he was 9, his mother took him to his first theater production. The box office man couldn't find any seats until his mother discovered an extra $5 in her purse. *"It's OK, son,"* she said. *"Everybody does it."*

When he was 12, he broke his glasses on the way to school. His Aunt Francine persuaded the insurance company that they had been stolen and they collected $75. *"It's OK, kid,"* she said. *"Everybody does it."*

When he was 14, Johnny and his family went to the movies. His father said, "Tell 'em your 13 to get the child's rate." *"It's OK, son,"* he said. *"Everybody does it."*

When he was 15, he made right guard on the high school football team. His coach showed him how to block and at the same time grab the opposing end by the shirt so the official couldn't see It. *"It's OK, kid,"* the coach said. *"Everybody does it."*

When he was 16, he got his first summer job at the local supermarket. His assignment was to put the over-ripe strawberries on the bottom of the box and the good ones on top where they would show. *"It's OK, kid,"* the manager said. *"Everybody does it."*

When he was 18, Johnny and a neighbor applied for a college scholarship. Johnny was a marginal student. His neighbor was in the upper 3% of his class, but he couldn't play right guard. Johnny got the scholarship. *"It's OK, son,"* his parents said. *"Everybody does it."*

When he was 19, he was approached by an upper classman who offered the test answers for $50. *"It's OK, kid,"* he said. *"Everybody does it."*

Johnny was caught and sent home in disgrace. *"How could you do this to your mother and me?"* his father said. *"You never learned anything like this at home."* His aunt and uncle were also shocked. *"If there's one thing the adult world can't stand, it's a kid who cheats."*

The Postscript (By Me)

When Johnny graduated from college with an accounting degree, got his first job with a major manufacturing company, and took his first business trip, he was told to be sure to *"round up"* on his expense report. *"It's OK, everybody does it."*

And, when Johnny was involved in his first quarter end close and revenues were short of forecast, he was told to pull some orders forward and show them as shipped. *"It's OK, everybody does it".*

Let's do a few more...

****

Suppose you *(or Johnny)* are on an online dating site. You are suspicious that most people are exaggerating their profile. Well, you are right. Research supports your suspicion. But...

"It's OK, everybody does it."

****

Have you heard the old joke about a lawyer who dies and goes to the Pearly Gates? St. Peter says to him, *"you only look about 45 years old."* *"Yes,"* says the lawyer, *"I just turned 45."* *"But our records of your billable hours would indicate you are 94 years old."*

"It's OK, everybody does it."

****

Dr. McCabe's graduate students claimed, *"Everyone was cheating"* and *"cheating was necessary to get ahead,"* as a rationalization for their actions.

I'll bet that most who did not return the *"lost"* wallet rationalized by saying to themselves, *"Not my fault; I didn't lose the wallet,"* or *"I bet if I lost my wallet, no one would return it."*

Okay, I'll get to the point now.

Psychological research clearly shows that we are not as ethical as we think we are. Sometimes we are conscious of our unethical conduct, but sometimes we are not. Studies consistently show that we behave contrary to our best intentions and rationalize our reasons.

Yes, we have an ability *(if you can call it an ability)* to maintain a belief, while simultaneously acting contrary to it. We are often hypercritical, judging others more harshly than ourselves when evaluating the same transgressions. There is often a widespread double standard – one set of rules for us, one set of rules for others. *Just think back to Johnny and his parents.*

So why do we often not see this ethically contrarian behavior in ourselves or others? Apparently, we have *"blind spots,"* just like Johnny's parents.

THE BLIND SPOTS AND RATIONALIZATIONS

Most of us behave ethically, *most* of the time. But very few of us behave ethically, *all* of the time. Sadly, some people don't recognize an ethical dilemma for what it is. But thanks to Max H. Bazerman and Ann E. Tenbrunsel, who wrote the book on the subject, we now know that we have *"blind spots." (Full book title: Blind Spots: Why We Fail To Do What's Right And What To Do About It.)*

We all have different life experiences. Money, authority, peers, groups, customers, and a multitude of conflicts of interest situations can lead to lack of objectivity *(i.e., a blind spot)* resulting in unethical conduct.

Then we rationalize our behavior and tend to ignore future consequences of our actions, particularly if there is no perceived or actual harm at the time.

> *"When our actions are more distant from the execution of the dishonest act, we find it easier to be dishonest."*
> – Dan Ariely

Let's go through a few examples to solidify the concept.

BLIND SPOT #1: MONEY

"Money makes the world go 'round." Or, better yet, money makes the world go *blind.* We often underestimate the monetary impact on our ethical decisions.

Dan Ariely's research shows us that test participants are more likely to lie/cheat when they are paid for performance, particularly when there is no way to detect the cheating.

Individual incentive plans within organizations are notorious for producing unethical conduct *(more on this topic in Chapter 9)*. The previously mentioned Wells Fargo customer account scandal not only included a few Big Me characters, but also included many smaller characters that were blinded to the fact that money was influencing their behavior. Or they simply rationalized that they needed the money so badly, it negated their poor conduct.

BLIND SPOT #2: LEADERS

It's not just money that blinds us. People will also engage in unethical behavior in order to fulfill formal or informal obligations to authority. This can be as simple as, *"I knew it was wrong, but my boss told me to do it."*

Can you think of a situation where ethical considerations were compromised to satisfy a leader or members of management? *I can.* I lived it for a very, *very* short period of time. When in public accounting, I had a "boss" tell me to *"fake it 'til you make it."* Needless to say, I am not good at faking anything, so that was short-lived.

> *"It is inexcusable to do something simply because a person ordered you to do it."*
> – Jocko Willink, Retired U. S. Navy SEAL

Take it from Jocko with twenty years of service *"rising through the ranks to become the commander of Task Unit Bruiser, the most decorated special operations unit of the Iraq War."* The military is obviously known for following orders through the chain of command, but there is an exception for illegal, unethical, or immoral conduct. There are no excuses *(rationalizations)* even in the military, even when given an order. So, you and I have no excuse.

BLIND SPOT #3: GROUP THINK

Group think, "*a tendency for cohesive groups to avoid a realistic appraisal of an alternative course of action in favor of unanimity,*" can also result in unethical conduct. The group think environment sometimes prevents individuals *(or small groups)* from challenging questionable, unethical decisions. It is called the context effect.

> "*We so fear exclusion from the group that we are willing to do things that we would find unconscionable in other circumstances.*"
> – David Brooks

We look to others to model our behavior. Sometimes the behavior is appropriate; other times – it's not. Dan Ariely's studies also show "*that cheating is infectious and can be increased by observing behavior of others around us.*"

I bet you can think of an example where you went along with the crowd and regretted it later. *(Think high school, y'all – everyone is doing it. And yes, I said y'all. I went to high school in the south.)*

BLIND SPOT #4: LEGALITY

The classic "legality" rationalization case comes from the former CFO at Enron, Andrew Fastow. Even though the facts clearly show rampant accounting fraud, for which he was convicted *(and went to prison)*, Fastow claimed that in part he felt the actions were justified *(rationalized)* because he never broke the rules (the U.S. Generally Accepted Accounting Principles) and the outside auditors, inside and outside attorneys, and the Board of Directors at the time approved his actions.

Per Fastow himself, *"You can follow all the rules and still commit fraud at the same time... When you're in the business world, it's a lot harder to recognize unethical situations than you think... our financial statements were intentionally misleading. But did I think that was wrong? No. I was just following the rules."*

I'm hopeful you agree that this is not an acceptable rationalization *(if there is such a thing)* for the inappropriate conduct, lack of ethical conduct, and accounting fraud at Enron. Nor is the blaming of others that approved the actions; perhaps they all fell into the "group think" or "leaders" blind spot traps as well.

"Laws define courses to which we must legally adhere or avoid. Ethics are standards of conduct that we ought to follow."
– Jon M. Huntsman

BLIND SPOT #5: CONFLICTS OF INTEREST

There is unambiguous evidence of the psychological aspects of conflicts of interest, meaning it undoubtedly can lead to another blind spot in our ethics.

Consider a typical cancer patient who receives advice from three prominent physicians, representing three specialties in cancer treatment: a surgeon, a radiologist, and a homeopathic physician. Would anyone be surprised that the respective physicians recommended a treatment protocol that was consistent with their area of specialization only?

*"Biased incentives can – and do –
lead even the most upstanding professionals astray."*
– Dan Ariely

The financial services industry is *full* of conflict situations. Are financial advisors and brokers looking out for investor interests or their own? Here is their *(sad and terrifying)* rationalization: I know I gave poor advice, but the customer/investors would have made even worse decisions on their own.

There is always a rationalization for acting in a self-serving, sometimes unethical, manner. Education, incentives, and personal preferences sometimes prevent objectivity, create a conflict of interest, and provide an ethical dilemma.

BLIND SPOT #6: CUSTOMERS

Lastly, often cited in discussions of ethics, is the 1986 Challenger space shuttle disaster. There was evidence of potential O-ring failure at low temperatures *(and there were unprecedented low temperatures on the morning of the launch)*. But pressure from NASA *(the customer in this case)* to launch trumped the judgement of Morton Thiokol engineers, who recommended not to launch.

This tragic case reminds us to beware of those pressures to perform or satisfy others, which can come from anywhere: customers, bosses, peers, etc., because they can overcome our ethical decision-making.

> *"Your actions are either praiseworthy or blameworthy."*
> – Gerald K. Harrison

BLIND SPOTS: GENERALLY SPEAKING

While the specific examples above are helpful in recognizing our potential blind spots, there are many others just lurking on the surface of "normal" life.

For example, organizational environments with a questionable culture or values can easily perpetuate unethical conduct *(it's called ethical and moral relativism)*. Employees rationalize and simply call the unethical decision a *"business decision."* Sadly, this is a very common rationalization in today's society.

Those who feel underpaid or unappreciated at organizations justify unethical conduct due to what they consider disrespectful treatment. They don't pay me enough for what I do, so I'll steal to make up the perceived difference. It's all neatly rationalized.

Self-preservation can be one of the most common blind spots and rationalizations of them all. It can easily overwhelm ethical considerations. Would you quit your job before doing something unethical? Or are you in the *"I thought I would lose my job"* rationalization camp?

And apparently, just getting away with unethical conduct makes it more blinding and addictive. Embezzlement starts out small and builds over time. Ponzi schemes start out as a simple, short-term, *"robbing Peter to pay Paul,"* then grow into a major fraud over time.

> *"Committing fraud and getting away with it can become addictive. Once one succeeds...*
> *it gets harder and harder to stop."*
> – Biegelman and Bartow

Put another way: *"Once we begin to cheat, even if only by a little, over time it can become a habit."* (Beautifully put, Dan Ariely.) I guess the flimsy rationalization is, if I got away with it once, I can and should do it again. Welcome to the mindset of Bernie Madoff and many other fraudsters.

> *"Small moral compromises on Monday make you more likely to commit other, bigger moral compromises on Tuesday."*
> – David Brooks

And lastly, the psychological distance between a dishonest act and its consequences all potentially contribute to increasing unethical conduct and blind spots.

Just think about a cashless society *(hello cryptocurrencies, like bitcoin, and even just debit/credit cards)* and working from remote locations with less person-to-person contact *(hello COVID-19)*. No victim that you or I know, or will ever know, makes it easier to lie, cheat, steal. But with no clear victim, it's an *"out of sight, out of mind"* world. The structural and societal changes and trends that create psychological distancing are only going to get more prevalent.

ADVERSITY AS A BLIND SPOT

Unfortunately, it has been highly noted that individuals compromise their ethics in times of adversity or challenge. They are more tempted to cut corners, take shortcuts, and engage in unethical behavior. You know – lie, cheat, steal.

Recall our previous discussion about Jon M. Huntsman, founder of Huntsman Chemical, who wrote the book *Winners Never Cheat*. We referred to Huntsman as someone who set firm ethical *"anchors"* in his life and business as described in the previous *Ethical Anchors* chapter. In the second version of his book, subtitled, *"Even in Difficult Times"* *(re-published in 2008 in response to the financial crisis),* he emphasized the temptation to behave differently when times are tough – as an individual, leader, or organization.

Huntsman begins the book with the comment that *"happiness is not the absence of conflict, but the ability to cope with it."* But he acknowledges what we all know; it is a lot easier to deal with adversity in good times than in bad times. The fears and stress of adversity can tempt even the most ethical, leaving them vulnerable to bad choices. Huntsman boils down ethics and adversity into a few principles:

> *"The adherence to an ethical code is best defined as how one honors a bad situation or a bad deal."*
>
> *"It is important... to settle on a set of values common to... most every instance."*
>
> *"Times change, situations change, lives change, technology changes. Situations may be altered; basic values may not."*

The temptation in bad times, professionally or personally, is to *"cook the books,"* weasel out of that contract, cheat on taxes, and, in general, look for an unfair, unethical advantage. Panic sets in and there is a tendency to *"deny and deflect"* and attempt to rationalize away the situation – to make it go away by *(I repeat)* taking shortcuts, cutting corners, or even worse – lying, cheating, stealing.

But to me, the real answer to avoid this, as outlined in my *Choices* book in chapter one: *"Choosing to Embrace Adversity,"* requires a specific course with four stages.

Stage 1: You have to recognize that adversity cannot always be anticipated or controlled but it can be accepted for what it is. *This is what I call the ethical acceptance stage.*

> *"We are all faced with a series of great opportunities brilliantly disguised as impossible situations."* – Chuck Swindoll

Stage 2: You have to reach out for support from family, friends, professional contacts, trusted advisors, and counselors. *This is the ethical advocate stage.*

Stage 3: You have to conduct an internal assessment of yourself or your organization, become more self-aware, and come to grips with your shortcomings. *This is the ethical assessment stage.*

Stage 4: You have to develop and execute a plan to modify behavior necessary to overcome the economic, health, societal, or other challenge you are facing in an ethical way. Re-focus at least part of your efforts externally to help others who are facing a similar adversity. Reframe your adversity to a newfound mission to ethically address similar issues and to serve others. *This is the ethical action stage.*

You have to move on. You can't look back on adversity and still continue on an ethical path for the future. You have to put all your energy on the door that is opening, not the door that is closing. You have to focus on the glass half full, not on the glass half empty. You have to adopt an *ethical growth mindset...* continuously learning and adapting in the face of unethical temptations.

The bottom line: don't turn to *unethical* behavior and rationalizations to face your adversity. Use *ethical* behavior to forge out of and beyond the adversity.

And remember, the ethical anchors in your life apply to good times and bad. As Huntsman states,

> *"...in the darkest of times,*
> *temptation will be the most alluring."*

"These are times for a mid-course pep talk, a reminder to stay the course, to run the good race, to fight the good fight, to follow the rules we learned long ago."

"They will see us through the hardships and help us make ourselves and the world better off."

And in the wise words of Martin Luther King Jr....

"The times are always right to do what's right."

When facing adversity or not...

Don't be an Ethical Rationalizer.

****

THE FINAL ETHICAL CHOICE:

THE EVERYDAY ETHICIST

What, exactly, is the road to The Everyday Ethicist? *I'm glad you asked.*

"You may not have had much control in shaping your circumstances, but you have the power to change your circumstances and thereby shape your [ethical] future."
– Blanchard/Peale

The road of The Everyday Ethicist is one where we *only* make ethical decisions. A road where we make decisions that are the result of thoughtful, reasoned reflection of our personal values.

"Individuals, without a doubt, have the power to influence the amount of duplicity in their lives and shape their speech and action."
– Sissela Bok

A road where we do what *should* be done. A road where we do *no harm* to others. It may sound simple, but the truth is it takes hard work. And it's time to take it seriously.

> *"The unexamined life is not worth living."*
> – Socrates

This is why I believe *"character choices"* are the most important choices that we will ever make.

> *"One's philosophy is not best expressed in words; it is expressed in the choices one makes."*
> – Eleanor Roosevelt

So, if you are ready to continue down the path to become The Everyday Ethicist, here are your choices:

➢ Recognize that everyone *(I mean everyone)* is vulnerable to unethical behavior. Do a self-assessment to recognize your specific environment and personal vulnerabilities. James Clear in *Atomic Habits* writes, *"it is easier to avoid temptation than to resist it."* And, remember, a little lie or a little cheating can become a bad habit over time. Trust, once compromised, is very hard to regain.

> *"It takes twenty years to build a reputation and five minutes to ruin it. If you think about that, you'll do things differently."*
> – Warren Buffett

➢ Develop your own personal value statement and a code of self-conduct as your guide. As Ariely says, *"establishing rules can safeguard ourselves from ourselves."*

➢ Keep it personal. Focus on your actions and the effect they have on others. Even though many activities today are much more distant geographically and virtually, keep in mind that somewhere, somehow, someone will be affected by your decisions. Don't trade short-term personal gain for long-term negative consequences for others.

➤ Think through and write down thoughts to get a clear, developed plan for honest actions. *"I think, therefore I am."* (Descartes). In the words of Samuel Johnson, *"the first step to greatness is to be honest."*

➤ Imagine an article on the front page of the Wall Street Journal describing your actions and determine if you could explain those actions without guilt to your boss, mentor, best friend, religious leader, spouse, partner, parents, or children.

➤ Visualize defending your actions in front of a judge or arbitrator. Remember, the Ben Horowitz book title, *What You Do Is Who You Are.* You will be judged by what you do. And, also remember, the road to hell is paved with good intentions *(proverb of unknown origin).* Intentions don't matter; actions do.

➤ Project ethical challenges into future situations and pre-commit to follow intended ethical guidelines. Dan Ariely, in his book *Predictably Irrational* in a chapter about self-control, describes experiments where students were given few guidelines for behavior compared to those who were given specific behavioral expectations. Not surprisingly, those who had guidelines performed more in line with behavior expectations. *Why?* Per Ariely, *"Because without pre-commitments, we keep on falling to temptation."*

➤ Review critical ethical decisions and alternative actions with personal mentors, professional colleagues, or trusted advisors before acting. Everyone can benefit from counsel and convention from outside parties, whether family, friends, mentors, or institutions. Ethical decisions should withstand review and analysis by professional peers as well as public scrutiny. And always remember and honor the code of ethics for your profession!

➤ Judge your own ethical decisions the way you would judge others, which is by their actual behavior *(not their intentions)*.

➤ Make decisions as if you had trusteeship, stewardship, or fiduciary responsibility *(whether legally required or not)* for the best interest of those impacted by your decisions. The Golden Rule never, ever fails.

> *"... sooner or later [you] have to confront your values. Then you're forced to separate what is right from what is merely legal."*
> – Tom Robbins

➤ Meet or exceed your commitments but do not overcommit or exaggerate. Be fact driven. It is much better if the truth beats what you say than if what you say falls short of the truth. And keep your promises even when it hurts *(thanks, John Maxwell)*.

➤ Professional conduct is defined as *"a commitment to the interests of clients (stakeholders), in particular, and society, in general."* Any conflicts between professional conduct and business conduct *(sales, revenue, profits)* must be reconciled in favor of the stakeholders. Professional conduct = ethical conduct.

➢ Think of your actions in a *"it's my own business"* context. Customers do not want to do business with an organization they do not trust; employees do not want to work for an organization they do not trust; investors do not want to invest in an organization they do not trust. Your life is your business, act accordingly to earn trust.

➢ Don't let an ethical challenge go to waste. Let every ethical crisis develop your character and strengthen your resolve to do the right thing. *"Within every obstacle is an opportunity to improve our condition"* (Ancient Zen Parable). It's *not* about doing what is easy; it *is* all about doing what's right. And, as psychologist Dr. Henry Cloud counsels, don't be *"too busy doing what we need to do to ever become who we need to be."*

➢ Be proud of your integrity; be a model for ethical conduct. Always walk the talk and encourage and inspire others to do likewise. Don't be swayed by admirers or detractors in the process of deciding and doing what is right.

➢ Spend time and energy on what is really important. Build your most important ethical assets of courage, honesty, and humility. Remember, *"being right does not necessarily lead to being victorious."* Your ego is what will lead to your downfall. Courage, honesty, and humility never will. *(thank you, David Brooks)*.

➢ Treat others better than they treat you. Look for every opportunity to make the lives of others better, particularly those who cannot help themselves and cannot help you. In other words, *pay it all forward.* Do not pursue happiness at the expense of others or profit at others expense. As suggested by Sissela Bok, ask *"Yes but"* questions when evaluating impact of actions.

> ➤ Always speak the truth, even if your voice shakes. Tell your friends and associates that you will speak and report the truth and that you expect truthfulness in return, regardless of consequences. Speak up and speak truth to power.

"Far more [than happiness] matters to us as human beings . . . than what we experience, no matter how pleasant."
– Robert Nozick

See Exhibit I in the Appendix for The Everyday Ethicist Contract. *Post it; live by it.*

And, see Exhibit II in the Appendix for the Checklist for Ethical Decision Making. *Post it; make decisions by it.*

It's worth repeating here that most people spend their life focusing on *"resume virtues"* – education and skill development to make money and advance our careers. But The Everyday Ethicist focuses on *"eulogy virtues"* – character and courage traits that will endure forever more.

And, if *(no... let's be honest... WHEN)* you come to the crossroads of life where you must choose the road of ethical conduct versus unethical conduct, remember to choose to act with integrity, *even if...*

Even if... it only costs two dollars.

Even if... it costs you a friend.

Even if... it costs you your job.

THIS IS THE EVERYDAY ETHICIST PROPOSITION.

Now that you know the path to personally Becoming The Everyday Ethicist, it's on to learning how to become The Everyday Ethical Leader.

EXPLORE YOUR PERSONAL ETHICS

Recall examples where the "Big Me" mentality has affected you. (Either your actions or other's actions)

Recall examples where you failed to live up to your values by being an "Ethical Rationalizer."

How did you feel when you (or others) acted as a "Big Me" or an "Ethical Rationalizer?"

How can you handle situations in the future when you fear a compromise in your values?

What are the core values that have gotten you through adversity?

What values (when ignored) contributed to your adversity?

At what point will you quit your job, get out of a relationship, etc., before you quit your ethics?

What are the cornerstones you need to work on to become "The Everyday Ethicist?"

CHAPTER FIVE:

THE EVERYDAY ETHICAL LEADER

AS YOU READ THIS CHAPTER, think of leadership in the broadest sense. You can be a board member, an executive, a member of middle management, a front-line supervisor, a project manager, a team captain, or an individual contributor that simply interacts with others... and you are a leader.

In all cases, you affect others and the messages and pitfalls are the same. As Bill George (more from George to follow) states in *The Discover Your True North Fieldbook*, *"any time you face a decision that impacts others, you are leading."*

But to start the leadership ethics and character conversation, let's first discuss some troubling data.

The latest Gallup Poll *(December 2019),* which asked U.S. adults to rate the honesty and ethical standards of various groups of leaders, found the following:

Thirty percent of business executives' ethics were rated low or very low. Only 20% rated executive ethics as high or very high. The rest were rated in the middle – average ethics. Who wants their ethics to be rated *average (or below)?* As the Apollo 13 astronaut reported, *"Houston, we have a problem!"*

The reasons may be found in the headlines of the not too distant past. Some we have already mentioned, as a case of a Big Me, but are worth repeating here. Some we haven't mentioned yet and are worth bringing to your attention.

> *"Management is doing things right;*
> *leadership is doing the right things."*
> – Peter Drucker

****

VW Boss Charged over Diesel Emissions Scandal

Martin Winterkorn was elevated to the position of CEO of VW in 2007 after leading the Audi subsidiary in a successful effort to challenge BMW in market share.

Winterkorn implemented a strategy to take on Toyota's world dominance by introducing improved marketing, product design, and operations. He achieved the goal of attaining the leading market share in 2015. Winterkorn also set extremely unrealistic objectives that are widely considered to be the fuel that led to a culture that instigated a worldwide emission scandal. So, I ask you...

Was Winterkorn an ethical leader?

What did the Board of VW think of the culture that was created under the leadership of Winterkorn? What do you think of the leadership of the Board in allowing a *"profit over purpose"* culture to persist that ultimately lead to such a scandal?

(Winterkorn denied responsibility but resigned (i.e., was fired) in 2015 in the middle of the emissions fraud scandal.)

****

FORMER HEAD OF WELLS FARGO BANNED FROM BANKING AFTER ROLE IN SCANDAL

Wells Fargo CEO John Stumpf had been the highly regarded CEO of the second largest bank in the U.S. since 2007.

In 2016, a massive fraud was discovered that involved the practice of opening phony accounts in customers' names and forcing unnecessary fees and products on customers. After much investigation, the bank's Board blamed its top management for creating and incentivizing an aggressive sales culture that led to the fraud. Thousands of employees were fired, and millions of fines paid. So, I ask you...

Was Stumpf an ethical leader?

What did the Board of Wells Fargo think of the culture that was created under the leadership of Stumpf? What do you think of the leadership of the Board in allowing a culture to persist that ultimately lead to such a massive fraud?

(Stumpf blamed the failures on a few bad employees but retired from the bank not long after being grilled by Congress about fraud at the bank under his watch.)

****

GULF OIL SPILL: BP CEO HAYWARD JUST CAN'T HELP BLAMING SOMEONE ELSE

CEO Tony Hayward's first reaction to the Deepwater Horizon oil rig explosion in the Gulf of Mexico that killed 11 men, was shock, then anger, then he blamed someone else. Hayward had been BPs CEO since 2007 when the explosion occurred in 2010.

Hayward was appointed CEO after BP had experienced serious safety issues at its facilities in North America. Hayward acknowledged the issues and was committed to fix BPs careless corporate culture. Three years later, the Horizon rig explosion occurred in an environment of poor safety practices. So, I ask you...

Was Hayward an ethical leader?

What did the Board of BP think of the culture that was created under the leadership of Hayward? What do you think of the leadership of the Board in allowing an unsafe culture to persist that ultimately lead to the massive oil spill and death of employees?

(Hayward blamed the failure on subcontractors but by mid 2010 had been replaced as CEO.)

****

BOEING CEO OUT AMID ONGOING 737 MAX SCANDAL

Dennis Muilenburg was CEO of Boeing when two 737 Max planes crashed within five months of each other, one in

Indonesia in 2017 and one in Ethiopia in 2018, killing a total of 346 people.

The evidence pointed to a flawed flight control system that forced both planes into uncontrollable nose dives. But Boeing initially defended the design and suggested pilot error was to blame for the crashes.

For decades, Boeing's reputation was second to none. And in air travel, reputation is everything. Then the crashes occurred. The situation was compounded by revelations that Boeing officials knew of the system flaws before the crashes and appeared to have downplayed the safety concerns. So, I ask you...

Was Muilenburg an ethical leader?

What did the Board of Boeing think of the culture that was created under the leadership of Muilenburg? What do you think of the leadership of the Board in allowing an unsafe aircraft to continue to fly amid evidence that Boeing was at fault for design flaws that contributed to the fatal accidents?

(Muilenberg resigned in December 2019 with the confidence in Boeing aircrafts left in the past.)

****

I have saved the worst for last... a family affair of failed, unethical leadership.

SACKLERS WITHDREW NEARLY $11 BILLION FROM PURDUE AS OPIOID CRISIS MOUNTED

The family behind the popular painkiller drug, OxyContin – three brothers: Arthur, Mortimer, and Raymond Sackler – founded Purdue Pharma in 1952. In the mid-1990s, Purdue began selling what amounted to morphine in a pill – a long-lasting, dangerous, narcotic pain reliever.

After aggressively marketing opioid products for many years and after many lawsuits and many deaths from opioid addiction, it has been found that Purdue misbranded OxyContin as *"safer and less addictive than it was."* But in the meantime, the Sackler family, many of whom were actively involved in the company leadership and oversight *(i.e., Board members)*, made a fortune.

Purdue filed for bankruptcy in 2019, basically because courts found that *"Purdue had created more liability to society than it was worth."* But, in a final act of unethical leadership, stories uncovered that the Sacklers withdrew $10.7 billion from Purdue as the company began to receive legal scrutiny over the last decade. So, I ask you...

Were the Sacklers ethical leaders?

What did the Board *(or at least the non-conflicted Board members along the way)* of Purdue Pharma think of the culture that was created under the leadership of the Sacklers? What do you think of the leadership of the Board in allowing the aggressive marketing and selling of opioids, and misleading of regulators and consumers of risks in light of the growing opioid epidemic, which resulted in many, many deaths?

(By early 2019, there were no Sackler family members in positions of company leadership or on the Purdue Pharma board. However, as a result of their actions over many years, in 2020, Purdue Pharma, plead guilty to federal criminal charges for its role in creating the nation's opioid crisis and will pay more than $8 billion in fines and penalties. Other lawsuits continue.)

****

Did these leaders gain the full trust of the people they were leading? Did they have the trust of their customers and investors that they would do the right thing? Given their ultimate fate, your answer is most likely a resounding *"no."* However, the sad part to me is, it took years, perhaps decades in some instances, to get to that *"no."*

> *"The glue that holds all relationships together, including the relationship between the leader and the led, is trust, and trust is based on integrity."*
> – Brian Tracy

But at least we now see what unethical leadership looks like. And, it is our chance to uncover the characteristics of true ethical leadership.

I'll start by saying ethical leaders don't just care about *where* they are going, they care about *how* they get there. They know that market share, revenue growth, profits, and "winning" doesn't mean anything when there is lying, fear, cover-up, fraud, and risking lives.

Before I give you my full list of *The Everyday Ethical Leader* qualities, I'll summarize thoughts and opinions from a variety of perspectives: psychologists, business leaders, and academics.

****

LEADERSHIP & INTEGRITY

Dr. Henry Cloud, psychologist, leadership coach, and bestselling author, has great thoughts about integrity and leadership. In his book, *Integrity: The Courage to Meet the Demands of Reality*, he first points out that leaders generally fail from the inability to *"gain the complete trust of the people they are leading."*

He goes out of his way to make sure all readers understand that when he talks about character and trust, he is not just talking about *"not having to audit the numbers."* What Dr. Cloud is talking about is the extra trust factor that can rally the troops over the long-term to produce expected outcomes and deal with problems.

Some think the *"extra"* is grit *(read Angela Duckworth's book, Grit)* or hard work and opportunity *(read Malcolm Galdwell's book, Outliers)*, but for Dr. Cloud it is all about character and trust characteristics. It is the ability to connect authentically with other people; it is about acknowledging and understanding concerns. It is about empathy.

> *"To care for anyone else enough to make their problems one's own, is ever the beginning of one's real ethical development."*
> – Felix Adler

It is *"being oriented toward the truth"* – believing that truth is the foundation of business and of society. Telling the truth when it counts, even when the truth is painful. Understanding that knowing the truth is the only way to be *"in touch with reality"* – what is really going on. And knowing that the truth is the only way to make sound decisions.

Leaders with integrity take criticism and face problems and failures straightforwardly. All organizations face problems; all leaders fail at times. Leaders that confront problems honestly and transparently are more likely to succeed in the end. As Dr. Cloud states, *"The consequences of deceit are usually greater than the ones of truth."* Note, all our unethical leadership cases contained some degree of dishonesty, deflection, or deceit.

Leaders with integrity are *"oriented towards transcendence."* They recognize that some things in life are simply more important than they are. They understand that they are not the center of the universe. People prefer leaders who have a larger *"mission for a greater good,"* where self-interest and ego are set aside. According to Dr. Cloud, leaders with integrity balance the needs of all stakeholders and put values above all else – including self.

Choose truth, integrity, and transcendence.

****

JOHN C. BOGLE IS BACK

We already know that John C. Bogle set solid ethical anchors, but as the founder and CEO of Vanguard for many years, he also set a great example for ethical leadership. Here's a story about Bogle's principled leadership to prove the point:

Bogle became interested in the investment industry in the 1950's when in college. He selected a study of the mutual fund industry as the topic for his college thesis.

After conducting his statistical research, he discovered that mutual funds *"can make no claim"* (which they were doing) of returns greater than long-term market averages. Further, he concluded the fees associated with investing *only negatively* affected investor returns. *The higher the fees, the lower the returns.*

To Bogle, this was an ethical and character issue. The traditional practice of the industry put the investment managers' interests before the investors.

After further ongoing study and years of experience in the investment industry, he founded Vanguard. The new *"mutual"* company put the interests of investors ahead of the fund managers by focusing on index funds and low fees and *honestly* serving the needs of investors. He destroyed the myth that professional managers as a group would enhance the returns of investors.

Bogle was tested by the powers-that-be in the investment industry at the time. He was told that if he proceeded with his mutual structure *(truly serving investor needs)*, he would *"destroy the mutual fund industry as we know it."*

Well, he did destroy a large portion that was *not* focused on investors' interests. And thank goodness he did.

So, let's put Bogle in Dr. Cloud's model for ethical leadership. Bogle had all the character and trust characteristics. Bogle clearly was *"oriented toward the truth."* Self-interest and ego were of no interest to Bogle. He was all about the higher mission of honestly serving the customers' interests, not his own. It was about putting values above all else. He faced criticism but succeeded in the end.

And, yes, people followed. Vanguard is an organization of 18,000 crew members *(a Bogle term from the beginning)* serving more than 30 million customers with $5.6 trillion of assets managed. It is the largest mutual fund company with a market share greater than its next three competitors. *(All 2019 data.)*

Again, my favorite Bogle quote says it all:

"What does it all mean if there is no honor and character?"

Bogle wrote 11 books in his lifetime and he had a lot to say about ethical leadership. Since Bogle's theme seems to be looking out for others, I called his style "Steward Leadership" in my *Choices* book. The following highlights Bogle's leadership lessons. Everyday Ethical *(Steward)* Leaders:

✓ *Look out for the interests of all others that their decisions affect.*

✓ *Add value to stakeholders' interests before personal or business interests.*

✓ *Keep it simple not to confuse or conceal the truth.*

✓ *Are trustworthy with facts, values, and commitments.*

✓ *Value character over wealth, fame, or power.*

Success is acting in others' best interests, never your own.

****

WHAT YOU DO IS WHO YOU ARE

Ben Horowitz, cofounder and partner at the venture capital firm Andreessen Horowitz is the author of bestsellers including a book with the title of this section: *What You Do IS Who You Are.* The theme of the book is obvious by the title.

Horowitz makes his points by telling stories of unusual historical characters from the genius behind a slave rebellion in Haiti to the samurai of Japan. What the events have in common are the creation of cultures that were *"based on actions, not words"* and all represented *"a commitment to explicit ethics and principled virtues."*

Horowitz starts the book by telling a story about a sales manager who was otherwise very successful but lied all the time

– a compulsive liar. As a result of his success *and* lying, it became okay to lie throughout the organization. Because, well, others copy what they think is rewarded.

So, Horowitz asked a series of questions that he thinks may be indicators of an organization's culture. No, he didn't say, read the organizations mission and value statements and you will find out. Instead he asked questions like:

o   *Is a phone call important enough to return today?*

o   *Is a document good enough or should it be better?*

o   *If I know something is badly broken, should I say something?*

o   *Do I have to be on time for meetings?*

o   *Is winning more important than ethics?*

His point is that an organization's culture is what it does, in big and little ways, every day. *"It's how they behave when no one is looking."* And the leader sets the culture by what is done, not what is said.

Horowitz says, *"Coaching, and not direction, is the first quality of leadership."* Brilliant. I often say internal auditors should be in the business of "coaching, not just catching" at their organization. But Horowitz does highlight the need to do some catching because if bad actions are ignored, they become the culture.

In the case of the Japanese samurai, they called their principles *"virtues"* rather than *"values"* on the basis that virtues are what you do, while values are *(supposedly)* what you believe. All of this got me thinking about two contrasting organizations that have been in the news because of *what they do.* Both are privately owned. One is GardaWorld and the other is Wegmans Food Markets.

GARDAWORLD VS. WEGMANS

GardaWorld, was founded by Stephan Crétier, a Canadian businessman and entrepreneur. He is the President and CEO of the company. Garda is a full service provider of security related services and has grown rapidly from its inception in 1995. It is now one of the largest privately held security providers in the world, generating revenues over $4 billion.

Garda's Mission is: *To make the world a safer place by protecting our clients' people and assets everywhere.*

Garda's Vision starts: *We envision a world in which our clients' people and assets are safe and secure.*

Garda's Values includes: *Our integrity is the moral force that drives everything we do, every day, and with everyone with whom we interact.* References are also made to trust, respect, responsibility, pride, community, commitment, accountability, mitigating risks, safety and safeguarding people and assets. All the right words.

But words also mentioned are *"ambitious," "confident"*, and *"urgency,"* which may be the source of their big problems.

There is a saying among corporate executives. *Don't do anything that would be an embarrassment to yourself, your family, and your company if described on the front page of the Wall Street Journal.* Well, it wasn't the WSJ, but a regional newspaper in Florida had a front page article about Garda headlined *"Moving Millions, Leaving Mayhem."* The critical question raised in the article was: *At what price has Garda grown?*

The newspaper reporters found plenty of evidence of poorly maintained and unsafe trucks and inadequately trained employees with unsafe driving practices. The article reported data that showed that Garda had the worst safety record in its industry resulting in many injuries and 19 deaths in about a ten year period.

Garda's statements talk a lot about safety but ethical leadership is not *"Leaving Mayhem."*

What you *do* is who you are.

****

By contrast, a recent headline for Wegmans Food Markets is,

"Wegmans Ranked No. 1 for Corporate Reputation"

Wegmans is a family owned supermarket chain with 98 stores in the Northeast and mid-Atlantic region of the U.S. In 2019, the company was ranked No. 1 for corporate reputation among the 100 most visible companies, according to a Harris poll and study, which included the ratings of thousands of customers.

The study evaluates multiple factors that drive reputation including character, trust, culture, ethics and citizenship.

"Ours is a family company, where we all work together to demonstrate the shared values that are important to our customers, the communities we serve and to each of us," said Colleen Wegman, president and CEO. For the record, Wegmans' values are the following:

- ➤ *We care about the well-being and success of every person.*

- ➤ *High standards are a way of life.*

- ➤ *We make a difference in every community we serve.*

➢ *We respect and listen to our people.*

➢ *We empower our people to make decisions that improve their work and benefit our customers and our company.*

Customers and the public in general make choices based on how a company operates – not just on what they make, or sell, or service, or, *say.* Wegmans' leaders clearly live their values.

What you do is who you are.

****

Horowitz says,

"Culture isn't a magical set of rules that makes everyone behave the way you'd like. It's a system of behaviors...."

"Who you are is how people talk about you when you are not around. How do you treat your customers? Can you be trusted?"

"Who you are is not the values listed on the wall. It's not your marketing campaign. It's not what you say..."

One more time, what you do is who you are.

****

INSPIRE MORE PEOPLE

S. Truett Cathy (1921 – 2014) was an American businessman and founder of the Chick-fil-A restaurant. He opened his first restaurant in a suburb of Atlanta in 1946 *(not far from where I grew up, I often brag – as well as often give out Chick-fil-A gift cards).* If you live in the U.S., you may have noticed, it has since grown into a successful chain of restaurants.

Cathy received many honors for his leadership including the U.S. Lifetime Volunteer Service Award, the Norman Vincent Peale Humanitarian Award, the Horatio Alger Award, and the

Simon Prize for Philanthropic Leadership, among many others. He has been described as a genuine example of the servant leader and in Cathy's own words, he spent a lifetime of *"inspiring more people."*

"You can make a difference by impacting others around you by the life you live day by day."

He is the author of five books including *Doing Business the Chick-fil-A Way*. The book gives a clear picture of Cathy's leadership philosophy and principles upon which he built Chick-fil-A into one of the largest and most respected restaurant chains *(over 2300 locations and $2 billion in revenue)*. The restaurants are universally admired both for their customer service and revenue per location, which is far in excess of any other chain. Cathy is a clear, very credible model for leadership success.

"Our philosophy of doing the right thing and doing things right is hardly ever the easiest solution.
It is, however, always the best solution."

Many talk of the shareholder or stakeholder model for business. Well, the Chick-fil-A model could best be described as the ethical and moral, family model. His consistent theme over the decades in business was to build and run the business so his family would be proud to continue the legacy. The legacy was, and is, serving others and being a model by what is said and, more importantly, what is done *(sound familiar?)*.

"Unexpected opportunities almost always carry with them the chance to be a faithful steward and to influence others positively."

Cathy talks a lot about priorities and keeping them in order. Cathy was committed to financial success and meeting his financial obligations, but he was even more committed to his principles.

The primary principle was to take care of his employees *(treat them like family)* and they will take care of the customers *(and treat them like family).* Cathy was committed to developing people and the well-publicized *"closed Sunday"* policy grew out of the desire to provide employees at least one day a week *"devoted entirely to family, worship, and personal pursuits."*

The good Baptist that Cathy was, the second principle is based on a bible verse, Proverbs 22:1, *"A good name is better to be chosen than great riches, and loving favor rather than silver and gold."* In other words, earn and maintain a good reputation for honoring commitments and service to others.

The third principle could very well be to select restaurant managers *(called operators)* and employees based on character traits and to *"treat them as we wished to be treated."* Chick-fil-A values the operators and the employees they select based on a criterion of *"honesty, integrity, commitment, and loyalty to customers and us."* Cathy's policy was to *"hire trustworthy people – then trust them."*

> *"It's amazing how much you can accomplish when you trust the people around you and they trust you."*

Cathy further states, showing his all-in character counts principle, *"Character traits are most important. Everything else can be learned."*

Cathy's next principle is community service – to *"have a good name in the community."* Chick-fil-A selects people that want to make a difference in their communities and provides them with the opportunities to do so.

Chick-fil-A is also so committed to the stewardship principles that it has a plaque at the corporate office entrance that states:

> *"To glorify God by being a faithful steward*
> *of all that is entrusted in us.*
> *To have a positive influence on all who come*
> *in contact with Chick-fil-A."*

Cathy states in his book his belief that *"Wall Street analysts are more interested in profits than they are in principles and people."* Chick-fil-A to this day is privately owned in order to not waiver from its character principles and desire to serve others, counting on its ability to meet financial obligations by following the principled, servant leadership model.

I have to believe one of Cathy's favorite stories in his book is about kindergarten children visiting the Chick-fil-A corporate office. When he asked the children what they wanted to be when they grew up, one said, *"When I grow up, I want to be like you."*

Cathy was a prototypical ethical leader that inspired others. All leaders would be well served following the Cathy model of principled, ethical leadership. As Cathy wrote,

> *"...be very careful what you say.*
> *More important... be careful what you do."*

****

AUTHENTIC LEADERSHIP

Bill George brings knowledge and thoughtfulness regarding leadership as a successful former chairman and CEO of Medtronic, as well as an academic. He now studies and teaches business and leadership at the Harvard Business School. His 2003 book, *Authentic Leadership*, is based on his life's leadership experiences and observations.

The book has become a highly respected classic on leadership. George is widely recognized as one of America's premier business leaders and *Authentic Leadership* one of the most important, insightful leadership books of our time. The following are the messages from the book, not surprisingly, starting with ethics:

⇒ *Authentic leaders have a conviction about ethics.* They have firm values. They *"know they are defined by their values and their character." "When their principles are tested, they refuse to compromise."* They believe that values must be constantly reinforced and consistently reflected in the actions of leaders.

⇒ *Authentic leadership is about honesty, devotion to customers, and stewardship of all other stakeholders' interests for the long-term.* Authentic leaders understand that excessive emphasis on shareholder value can be misplaced and shareholder value ultimately only comes from serving customers. They understand that all stakeholders must be served for the overall organization to be successful.

⇒ *Authentic leaders have a strong sense of purpose.* They know why they do what they do. *"Others follow them because they know where they stand."*

⇒ *Authentic leaders overcome obstacles.* They are *"able to stand alone against the majority,"* if necessary to do the right thing. They are consistent and self-disciplined. They convert their values into consistent actions. They *"walk the talk."*

⇒ *Authentic leaders build relationships.* These relationships not only connect them with others but also others with each other. They understand that *"it is the openness and the depth of the relationship with the leader that trust and commitment is built."*

⇒ *Authentic leaders have a balanced life.* Because *"balanced leaders develop healthier people and organizations."* They understand that people who let business dominate their lives expect others to do the same, which is unreasonable and unrealistic.

Leaders according to George have...

"the ability to ignite the souls of their employees to achieve greatness far beyond what anyone imagined possible."

Ethical leaders are authentic leaders.

****

TOTAL ETHICAL MANAGEMENT

W. Edwards Deming (1900 – 1993) is considered the founding father of Total Quality Management (TQM). He and his concepts helped support the turnaround of Japan's post-World War II economy, particularly the automotive and electronics industries.

Later, the adoption of Deming's TQM principles helped rejuvenate the manufacturing industry in the United States.

Most successful companies use Deming principles in their management today although many call it something else. It could be called, just as appropriately, Total Ethical Management (TEM).

Deming understood that the intense focus on short-term output goals can and often resulted in ethical compromises. He understood the importance of ethical conduct in ensuring production of high quality products and providing quality services to meet customers' needs.

Deming taught that a code of ethical conduct was essential to reduce the frequency of unethical behavior, by reducing its acceptability. To Deming, the way to *"quality"* was *(and still is)* by ethical behavior.

In the spirit of Deming, William Stimson, Ph.D. in systems engineering and the author of many books on quality auditing, has a proposed code of ethics for business management worth repeating. I have shortened it to *"cut to the chase:"*

√ *Identify customer expectations and meet them.*

√ *Be open and honest with all.*

√ *Assume responsibility for quality, reliability, and safety of products and processes.*

√ *Inform all stakeholders of possible conflicts of interest.*

√ *Respect confidentiality.*

√ *Respect freedom of all to identify non-conformances.*

√ *Ensure all statements, reports, data, and certifications are true and complete.*

√ *Maintain a culture that encourages the ethical conduct of all.*

Late in his life, Deming was once asked how he would like to be remembered. He said:

> *"If at all... as someone who spent his life trying to keep America from committing suicide."*

The comment seems prophetic to me. Ineffective, unethical leaders all over the place – who have not followed the *"roads"* paved by Dr. Henry Cloud, John C. Bogle, Ben Horowitz, S. Truett Cathy, Bill George, and W. Edwards Deming – have destroyed *(or at least damaged)* their organizations to the detriment of themselves and their stakeholders.

There is no quality without ethics.

****

There is plenty of good advice on leadership choices offered by these leadership greats. Although there are several common themes, each offers a slightly different perspective for a leader who is effective *and* ethical. And I believe all combined are key ingredients of successful leaders.

But wait one minute.

We aren't finished yet on the road to becoming *The Everyday Ethical Leader.*

There is one more group that has a lot to offer... and I happen to really, *really* like this group.

****

THE WOMEN OF ETHICAL LEADERSHIP

This is not a debate whether women are more ethical than men. But it is an opportunity to highlight the ethical leadership of women throughout history *(and today),* to emphasize the qualities that set them apart, and to learn from them.

Remember, Harriett Tubman? Well, there's a lot more to the story.

Harriet Tubman
1822 – 1913
Civil war scout, spy, nurse, civil rights activist

Harriett Tubman *(born Araminta Ross)* was born into slavery and became an American abolitionist and political activist.

Tubman was beaten and whipped by her various masters as a child in Maryland. However, in 1849, Tubman escaped to Philadelphia. She then immediately returned to Maryland and, subsequently led 13 missions to rescue approximately 70 enslaved people including family and friends using anti-slavery networks and safe houses.

During the American Civil War, she first served as a cook and a nurse, then as an armed scout and spy for the Union Army. Tubman was the first woman to lead an armed expedition in the war and she guided a raid that led to the liberation of more than 700 slaves.

After the war, she returned to the family home on property she had purchased in 1859 in Auburn, New York, where she cared for her aging parents and many others. Even though she was illiterate, Tubman traveled to New York City, Boston, and Washington, D.C. where she spoke on behalf of the women's suffrage movement working alongside women such as Susan B. Anthony. She once said,

"Every great dream begins with a dreamer. Always remember, you have within you the strength, the patience, and the passion to reach for the stars to change the world."

When her health began to deteriorate, she moved into her namesake rest home for elderly African Americans that she established in 1911. She died in 1913 at age 91.

She is an icon of courage and the epitome of ethical leadership.

Next, at the other end of the social-economic-political spectrum was...

Eleanor Roosevelt
1884 – 1962
American political figure, diplomate, activist

Anna Eleanor Roosevelt served as the First Lady of the United States from 1933 to 1945, during her husband President Franklin D. Roosevelt's four terms in office.

Eleanor Roosevelt was a member of the prominent American Roosevelt and Livingston families and a niece of President Theodore Roosevelt. With exposure to politics and public affairs her entire life, she resolved to seek fulfillment in leading a public life of her own.

Roosevelt regularly made public appearances on her husband's behalf, and as First Lady, she significantly reshaped and redefined the role. She was a controversial First Lady at the time for her outspokenness, particularly on civil rights for African-Americans.

She was the first presidential spouse to hold regular press conferences, write a daily newspaper column, write a monthly magazine column, host a weekly radio show, and speak at a national party convention. And on occasion, she publicly disagreed with her husband's policies.

She advocated for expanded roles for women in the workplace, the civil rights of African Americans and Asian Americans, and the rights of World War II refugees.

Following her husband's death in 1945, Roosevelt remained active in politics for the remaining 17 years of her life. She pressed the United States to join and support the United Nations and became its first delegate. She served as the first chair of the UN Commission on Human Rights and oversaw the drafting of the Universal Declaration of Human Rights.

Later, she chaired the John F. Kennedy administration's Presidential Commission on the Status of Women. By the time of her death, Roosevelt was regarded as...

"one of the most esteemed women in the world."

...and yet another pillar of ethical leadership from the past.

And, now there is...

Margrethe Vestager
Born 1968
Danish politician, European commissioner

Margrethe Vestager was born in Glostrup, Denmark, the daughter of Lutheran ministers. She studied at the University of Copenhagen, graduating in 1993 with a degree in Economics.

Vestager is a Danish social liberal politician, Executive Vice President of the European Commission (EU) for a Europe Fit for the Digital Age and the European Commissioner for Competition. She was the political leader of her party in Denmark from 2007 to 2014, and served as Minister of Economic Affairs and the Interior from 2011 to 2014.

Within a few months of assuming her European Commissioner role in 2014, she brought antitrust charges against Google. The EU commission had initially opened the investigation into Google in 2010, and had reached a settlement deal with Google by 2014 but was unable to convince the European Commission to accept it.

Vestager inherited the case and showed a great desire to continue pursuing Alphabet (Google) over the alleged antitrust violations. Also, she initiated investigations into the tax affairs of Fiat, Starbucks, Amazon, and Apple.

In 2014, she launched proceedings against Gazprom, one of Europe's main gas suppliers, over allegations of breaching EU antitrust rules by putting in place artificial barriers to trade with eight European countries. And, in 2015, Vestager ordered Cyprus Airways to pay back over 65 million euros(€) in illegal state aid received in 2012 and 2013 as part of a restructuring package.

In 2016, after a two–year investigation, Vestager announced Apple Inc. received illegal tax benefits from Ireland. The Commission ordered Apple to pay a fine of €13 billion, plus interest, in unpaid Irish taxes.

In 2017, Vestager ordered Amazon to pay €250 million of back taxes, and in 2018, the EU Commission fined Qualcomm €997 million for allegedly abusing its market dominance.

In 2018, she fined Alphabet (Google) €4.3 billion for entrenching its dominance in internet searches by illegally tying together their service and other mobile apps with Android.

In 2019, she fined Mastercard €570 million for preventing European retailers from shopping around for better payment terms. Also, in 2019, Vestager ordered Google to pay a fine of €1.49 billion for abusive practices in online advertising.

She has been described as...

"the rich world's most powerful trustbuster."

...and is yet other example of strong ethical leadership.

And, lastly, a strong and accomplished person that has become very familiar to us all recently...

Dr. Deborah Birx, M.D.
Born 1956
American physician and diplomat who served as the response coordinator for the White House Coronavirus Task Force

Deborah Birx was born in Pennsylvania. She majored in chemistry at Houghton College and then earned her medical degree from the Hershey School of Medicine at Pennsylvania State University. Birx served as a physician in the United States Army, rising to the rank of colonel.

Birx was on the frontline against a mysterious virus which scientists couldn't stop. It was the 1980s and Birx was fresh out of medical school. The virus was HIV.

In 1980, she began her medical career in internal medicine clinical immunology at the Walter Reed Army Medical Center and the National Institutes of Health. Her career as a clinician in immunology was focused on HIV/AIDS vaccine research.

At the medical center where Birx worked as a US army physician, healthy young men were dying in droves from an illness no one could name. Birx turned the heartbreak and confusion into research and treatment. In doing so, she embarked on a career dedicated to stopping HIV and AIDS.

From 1985 to 1989 she served as an assistant chief of the hospital immunology service in the Department of Allergy and Clinical Immunology at Walter Reed.

From 1996 to 2005, she was the Director of the United States Military HIV Research Program at the Walter Reed Army Institute of Research helping lead HIV vaccine clinical trials.

After retiring from military service, Birx served as the director of CDC's Division of Global HIV/AIDS, part of the agency's Center for Global Health, from 2005 to 2014.

In 2014, Birx became the United States Global AIDS Coordinator. Her role as ambassador is to help meet the HIV prevention and treatment U.S. targets set to end the AIDS epidemic by 2030.

For her efforts overseeing a program responsible for the fight against HIV resulting in saving millions of lives, Birx has been called a legend in the global health community.

Birx is also a member of the Board for Global Fund to Fight AIDS, Tuberculosis and Malaria.

Beginning 2020, she became the White House Coronavirus Task Force coordinator. In her role as coronavirus response coordinator, she became one of the most prominent voices around this crisis and to me, she is...

An ethical leader and, in this fight, a real standout.

Whether it is rescuing slaves, advocating for the rights of disadvantaged Americans, taking on the powerful, or fighting diseases, the sixty-four thousand dollar question...

ARE WOMEN LEADERS MORE ETHICAL THAN MEN? AND, IF SO, WHY?

In 2018, the Pew Research Center studied leadership *"traits and competencies and how they intersect with gender."*

They found that *"many, if not most, Americans see men and women as equally capable when it comes to some of the key qualities and behaviors that are essential for leadership. Being honest, holding up under pressure and standing up for what they believe in are some examples of traits that are viewed as essential for leaders in both politics and business and areas where majorities of the public say neither gender has the upper hand."*

In addition, a *majority* say male and female leaders have different leadership styles, and *few* think one gender has a better overall approach than the other.

But, for those who *do* see a difference between male and female leaders, they see the female difference as *"being compassionate and empathetic and being able to work out compromises."* And, for those that see a difference, women are perceived as stronger at *"being honest and ethical"* and better at *"standing up for what they believe in."* One-third as many thought that men are better at honesty, ethics, and courage *(my term, not a technical one)* qualities.

So, the perception gives a slight edge to women when it comes to ethics related characteristics. Men get the edge when it comes to risk taking, which I could argue might relate to unethical conduct.

When asked which gender is best at creating a safe and respectful workplace, the survey showed that 43% say female business leaders do a better job; only 5% say male leaders are better in this area.

Female business leaders are also seen as having a relative advantage over their male counterparts when it comes to valuing people from different backgrounds (35% say women are better at this, 3% say men are better); considering the impact business decisions have on society (33% vs. 8%); providing guidance or mentorship to young employees (33% vs. 9%); and providing fair pay and good benefits (28% vs. 5%).

In business, creating a safe and respectful workplace is on par with honesty and ethics; 89% say it's essential for a business leader to be able to do this. On honesty, ethics, and safety, those who see a difference between men and women view women as better equipped.

So, I would conclude from the data that although there is no difference in the perception of overall effectiveness of leaders based on gender, *there is a least a slight edge favoring female leaders in promoting ethics in the workplace.*

So, what can we learn from this analysis?

If the generic makeup of women actually gives even a slight edge in favor of ethical leadership, I believe we should try to emulate those traits.

Here are the (simple) gender stereotypes:

- Feminine traits include gentleness, empathy, humility, and sensitivity.
- Masculine traits include strength, courage, independence, and assertiveness.

If we want to tip the scale toward ethical leadership, we need to consider the whole list, the whole package.

Women: Keep on doing what you are doing. Do what comes naturally with empathy and sensitivity, which seems to show up with more honesty and better ethical decision making. Just start doing it more courageously and assertively.

Men: Try to move from your natural tendency of risk taking and assertiveness and recognize its potential impact on your ethical *(or unethical)* decision making. And, start working on your empathy and humility.

Everyone: Be strong and show empathy. Be assertive and show sensitivity. Lead with integrity, courage, and humility and model the ethical leadership traits of Harriett Tubman, Eleanor Roosevelt, Margrethe Vestager, and Dr. Deborah Birx –

The Women of Ethical Leadership.

****

Before we wrap up this section up, I have to mention on last thing. In doing research for this book, I noticed a distinct lack of female book authors on ethics.

So, I conducted a completely unscientific study by searching the web for female authors of books related to ethics.

The result:

> *Of the first 32 ethics books that popped up, 27 were written by males. Four were written by females; one was co-authored by a male and female.*

What does this prove?

> *Probably nothing.*

But I do suppose it is a little ironic that men, who seem to not do quite as well at ethics, are writing all the books on ethics. Nonetheless, I at least have the satisfaction of adding to the minority as a female author of a book on ethics.

****

The American Institute of Certified Public Accountants (AICPA), the Association of Certified Fraud Examiners (ACFE), the Institute of Internal Auditors (IIA), and many other professional organizations refer to *"tone at the top"* when discussing the importance of leadership regarding ethics.

In my opinion, the most important responsibility of senior executives *(and all other leaders)* is creating a culture of honesty and integrity. Most people act according to the example set by their leaders. And, no leader can expect that their subordinates will act ethically when the leader does not.

> *"The greatest leaders... studied throughout all our research cared as much about values as victories...."*
> – Jim Collins

As a part of my training programs, primarily for auditors and accountants, I conduct a survey regarding their opinions about ethics and leadership in their respective organizations. Thousands have participated in the survey representing various organizations and industries. I ask the participants to rate their organizations relative to the following statements:

- *Leaders don't seem to care about ethical standards and ethics.*

- *Leaders sometimes exhibit unethical conduct.*

The scores can range from a perfect score (A) to pretty darn bad (F). On that five-level scale, the statements both typically rate a solid "C."

During my live webinars, I also ask a polling question regarding leader ethics. *"Is ethics a top priority of leaders in your organization?"* There are three choices for responses. One-third responds *"Yes, ethics is No. 1."* About half respond *"Ethics crosses leaders' minds, sometimes."* And 16% respond that ethics is an *"afterthought"* for their leaders.

The real questions from this data:

- *Why do leaders feel it is okay to rate less than an "A" when it comes to caring about ethics and acting ethically?*

- *Why is ethics not a top priority of leaders?*

I'm not sure we have the answers. But what I do know is this; it is a sad reality that we need to overcome.

So, I ask you, how would your subordinates' rate you? What do you need to do/change to be perceived as an *Everyday Ethical Leader?*

THE EVERYDAY ETHICAL LEADER

My perspective of leadership is derived from thoughtful observations during my academic education *(Bachelors and Master's in Accounting)* and professional education *(Certified Public Accountant, Certified Internal Auditor, and Certified Fraud Examiner),* as well as my time as a Big Four auditor, a director of an Internal Audit function, a professor of higher education, and as an entrepreneur.

But more importantly, it is derived from both my genuine experiences of being led and of leading others. It came from working for someone from whom I learned nothing as well as from someone I learned much. It came from being self-employed (working for myself). It came from real-life, in the trenches, learning from mistakes, celebrating what works, and leadership practice. It came from taking the time to build a leadership philosophy, communicating that philosophy, and genuinely living and leading by that philosophy *every* day.

I will try not to overlap too much with the experts and role models; however, the following are my collective suggestions for what I call *"The Everyday Ethical Leader."* See Exhibit III in the Appendix for **The Everyday Ethical Leader Checklist.** *Print it, post it, lead by it.*

❖ *A genuine ethical leader is a model for ethical behavior and inspires others to do likewise.* They know that individuals tend to act the way leaders talk, so they talk about ethics and act accordingly. They know that one *"white lie"* can send a signal that hypocrisy is OK and open the floodgates for lying, falsification, and misrepresentation.

❖ *A genuine ethical leader is never a "lapdog."* The term may be offensive – if so, I apologize. However, almost every scandal seems to have a *"lapdog individual,"* or maybe even an entire *"lapdog department."* The CFO at Enron was one. Bernie Madoff had one. You *may* be tested in big ways; you *will* be tested in many small ways. Be prepared to report ethical and policy violations *(by anyone)* to whoever it takes to get the message out, and if necessary, resign. Your reputation is more important than a job.

❖ *A genuine ethical leader loves their whistleblowers.* They provide safe mechanisms to report ethics, conduct, values, and policy violations. They foster open communication between leadership and all stakeholders without fear of retaliation. They listen to everything, even the things that aren't fun to hear. They have more than an open-door policy; they have a *no-door* policy. They are prepared to sort through all the non-serious issues to find the one issue that is really critical to the future of their organization.

❖ *A genuine ethical leader never lets a crisis go to waste.* They let every crisis develop their character and the character of their employees, associates, and their organization. When a crisis occurs *(health and welfare, ethical, financial, operational, etc.)* they take timely, definitive action and communicate to all in the organization to reinforce the seriousness. Heightened awareness, particularly of ethical issues, is a learning opportunity.

❖ *A genuine ethical leader knows professional conduct trumps business conduct.* In the basic sense, business standards of behavior are simply to make money and not break the law. A genuine ethical leader doesn't believe this is good enough. They apply a professional conduct framework of respect and integrity for *all* stakeholder interests. Remember what I said previously on the road to becoming The Everyday Ethicist, *"any conflicts between professional (ethical) conduct and business conduct must be reconciled in favor of the stakeholders (professional conduct)."* Integrity comes first.

❖ *A genuine ethical leader doesn't overcommit or exaggerate.* It is much better that the truth beats what you say than if what you say falls short of the truth. Genuine ethical leaders are fact driven based on observations, data, logic, analysis, and reason, and are objective and impartial. They are aware of potential exaggerations and embellishments. They ensure they accurately commit and deliver on their commitments, and they teach others to do the same. *They believe a promise is a promise.*

❖ *A genuine ethical leader provides a moderating influence and a reality check on unrealistic goals and objectives.* They do not perpetuate the lie of an unrealistic goal that often results in cutting corners, shortcuts, compromises, and fudging the results. They are not swayed into making bad decisions based on relationships and/or financial incentives. They are prepared to focus resources on process, controls, quality, and overall checks and balances.

❖ *A genuine ethical leader "delivers their function" by observing and listening to the needs of their stakeholders.* They meet one-on-one with employees, they hold skip level meetings, they utilize surveys and obtain feedback however possible *(yes, they even just walk around!)* to find out what is *really* going on at their organization or function. They are transparent in knowledge and actions. They are vulnerable and admit mistakes. They develop meaningful personal and professional relationships. They mentor others.

Ethical leaders focus more on *coaching* employees to do the right things than *catching* employees doing the wrong things.

Ethical leaders understand that the downside risk caused by bad ethical decisions is greater than all the other good decisions put together.

And to paraphrase Dr. Henry Cloud, leaders with integrity look out for others interests when *they* are not looking.

Most think that the problem with unethical leaders is that they betray their shareholders. But I believe, first and foremost, they betray their families, then their communities, employees, customers and other associates. If leaders viewed the world from this perspective, maybe they would reconsider their actions.

THIS IS THE EVERYDAY ETHICAL LEADER PROPOSITION.

Now, we continue our journey to learn about The Everyday Ethical Organization. But, first, let's see what an (un)ethical organization looks like.

EXPLORE YOUR ETHICAL LEADERSHIP

What are the most important factors in being an ethical leader?

How do you show others that you "walk the talk" in regard to ethics?

What are your qualities that influence others to want to follow your lead?

What are your qualities that have driven others away?

Do others trust you? Why or why not?

How do you make others feel during a crisis? How are your crisis management skills?

Some leaders are prone to abuse of power. Describe your struggles in this area.

In what ways do you help others to become more effective ethically? What could you do to help more?

Do you have an ethical mentor? Are you an ethical mentor?

Are you constant and steadfast when it comes to ethical decisions (or are you sporadic and unpredictable)?

What is your ethical leadership philosophy going to be? What is your plan to communicate your philosophy?

CHAPTER SIX:

(UN) ETHICAL ORGANIZATIONS

(DENY, DEFLECT, DECEIT)

IF YOU WANT TO know how to fine tune your skills at running an unethical organization, this chapter is for you. *(Yikes, I hope not.)*

But, seriously, we all know that hindsight is 20/20 and we should be learning from past organizational mistakes. So why, then, does data show we aren't getting much better at deterring unethical conduct year over year?

The ACFE reported in its 2018 Global Study on Occupational Fraud and Abuse that the average organization loses 5% of its annual revenue to fraud. The 5% loss has been constant for years. You can do the math for your organization, but in aggregate for the world, that is a huge number.

Based on the 2018 report of the Ethics and Compliance Initiative, 22% of employees surveyed reported that they perceived some form of pressure to compromise or violate organization standards of business ethics. And one-third of employees reported that they had observed misconduct at work. To make things even worse, the report indicated that 36% of employees who had communicated the misconduct to their management suffered some form of retaliation.

I have conducted a Workplace Ethics Survey of my own with thousands of my training participants *(auditors, accountants, and other risk and finance professionals)* and only 3% of those surveyed responded that there were *no* ethical issues in their respective organizations. *Interested in taking the survey for yourself?* See Appendix V for the QR code/link to access the **Workplace Ethics Survey.**

Based on all the research and statistics, I don't think we need any more justification to make a big deal about organization ethics. It is time to determine what can be done to promote high ethical organization standards and prevent, or at least reduce, the amount of illegal, unethical, or immoral conduct.

I don't believe anyone takes a job with the intention of doing the wrong thing. A premise of W. Edwards Deming's TQM teachings was *"No one goes to work to do a bad job."* However, I believe that organizations have the ability of turning good employees into bad and making marginal employees worse *(hence why this chapter exists).* Fortunately, organizations can also do the opposite – make everyone even better, ethically and otherwise. And I promise we will discuss this positive side in later chapters.

> *"Never underestimate the power of the environment you work in to gradually transform who you are."*
> – David Brooks

We have already explored the importance of ethical leadership in the previous chapter and outlined what good leaders can do to promote ethical conduct within the organizations that they lead. Leadership cannot be underestimated as a major driver of conduct but there are many structural, behavioral, process, and environmental factors that also come into play.

So, let's first explore why organizations act unethically. What goes wrong? Aside from unethical leaders that have a self-serving financial or power motive, I believe organizations act unethically because of something usually called *culture.* Certainly *culture* is a function of leadership, but I think the group motives and behaviors are much more complex.

To help in the process, I have listed the Seven Deadly Sins of Organizations: *Pride, Greed, Lust, Envy, Gluttony, Wrath, Sloth.* Okay, just kidding, it's not those exactly – but close. The organization sins are:

➢ Deny And Deflect

➢ Disingenuous Leadership

➢ Move Fast and Break Things

➢ The Smartest Guys In The Room

➢ The Lawyers And Auditors Approved It

➢ Everyone Does It, So It Must Be OK

➢ Everything Is Grey

All have to do with group motives, rationalizations, and mentality that can lead to overall unethical organization behavior. Kind of like the Big Me's of organizations.

You will note that organizations that have unethical tendencies suffer from many of these "sins" and there is overlap from one to another. Bad habits come in bunches and don't fit into nice neat categories. However, all seem to have a common element of short-term gratification *(financial or otherwise)* at the expense of long-term, negative consequences and, most importantly, the destruction of trust. For each of these organizational sins, think about the consequences and the resulting loss of trust of consumers, employees, investors, and society in general.

****

DENY AND DEFLECT

First, there are the organizations that adopt the *"not our fault"* mentality. No matter the reasons for or consequences of actions, the organization denies and deflects responsibility for the behavior. There is always a rationalization for the unethical conduct.

Think about the initial reaction of the tobacco industry as the evidence and pressure mounted regarding the harmful effects of smoking. The industry hid behind the *"not our fault"* claim for decades. *"Not our fault"* that we knowingly manufactured and marketed tobacco products for years after clear evidence that the products were/are harmful to their customers. Even though consumers were inundated by tobacco product advertising, the rationalization was – we didn't make anyone use the tobacco products. *Not our fault. Deny, deflect.*

We have already discussed leadership at Boeing. The initial reaction at Boeing was – not our fault that the two Boeing aircrafts crashed. Per Boeing, the fault lay with the inadequate training of the pilots by the airlines. *Not our fault. Deny, deflect.*

Then there is Johnson & Johnson (J&J) that aggressively marketed opioid pain killers to the degree that a judge in a lawsuit stated that J&J actions created *"...imminent danger and menace..."* to the citizens of Oklahoma. Of course, J&J's reaction was that it was not their fault. Regardless of J&J's sales and marketing techniques *(that were judged to be deceptive by the court),* they appealed the court's decision claiming first and foremost that opioid overdose deaths are the fault of the doctors and patients. J&J didn't force consumers to take the drugs. *Not our fault. Deny, deflect.*

The headline of a November 2018 New York Times article was *"Delay, Deny, and Deflect: How Facebook's Leaders Fought Through Crisis."* Instead of immediately acknowledging legitimate issues regarding the violation of privacy rights of users and how their personal information is shared as well as problems associated with the dissemination of information, Facebook's executives chose to delay, deny, and deflect. Rather than proactively fixing the issues, the instinct was to *"ignore warning signs"* and *"conceal them from public view"* according to the Times article. Facebook fought critics and regulators and placed blame on others. *Not our fault. Deny, deflect.*

Note, under duress and after a fine of $5 billion, Facebook ultimately changed its tune and the CEO announced that Facebook would make *"major structural changes"* to how it builds its products and conducts business. It's almost two years later as I am writing this, and I still have to say, *"we'll see."*

And how about Fabrice Tourre, the Goldman Sachs trader who was found guilty of mortgage fraud – misleading investors about sub-prime mortgage securities? At the time of the illegal conduct, he wrote a friend an email stating, *"...not feeling too guilty about this, the real purpose of my job is to make capital markets more efficient and ultimately provide the U.S. consumer with more efficient ways to leverage and finance himself, so there is my humble, noble, and ethical reason for my job."* I suppose it was said sarcastically but it's an approach taken often on Wall Street to deflect issues. *Not our fault. Deny, deflect.*

> *"Business is an establishment that gives you the legal, even though unethical, right to screw the naïve...."*
> – W. C. Fields

It's almost too easy to rationalize unethical conduct and that is why many organizations do it. There is no incentive to act ethically when *"deny and deflect"* is such an effective strategy – at least for a while.

"Not our fault" organizations are a free for all for marginal, if not downright unethical, behavior because the fall back positon can always be – blame someone else, deflect and deny responsibility. But, just remember, it never ends well.

****

DISINGENUOUS LEADERSHIP

"Ethics and oversight are what you eliminate
when you want absolute power."
– DaShanne Stokes

Then there is the organization with *"disingenuous leadership."* Those organizations may have all the proper value statements posted on the website *(and perhaps even the wall)* but their leaders do not *"walk the talk."* Integrity is all for show; it is all form over substance. The *"talk"* or *"form"* is a smoke screen for all out financial self-interest – personal wealth, organization growth, profits, and power.

Then there is an example of not even having the *"form"* in place when it comes to ethics values. Brian Chesky, a co-founder and the current CEO of Airbnb, is quoted in a Stanford University speech as saying *"integrity, honesty – those aren't core values. Those are values that everyone should have."* Okay, maybe that's true, but in today's world – especially after reading about all the "Big Me" examples – do we really think that is a logical argument? Sadly, I think we need to be more explicit within our organizations about our ethics values.

So, the real question is, what *are* Airbnb's values in regard to ethics and integrity, since they don't explicitly state them? Is Chesky being disingenuous by "saying" everyone should act with honesty and integrity, but perhaps Airbnb as an organization doesn't have to?

We know that Airbnb has exploded in popularity; however, most now also recognize that they are anything but ethical by normal business standards. Airbnb is a facilitator of hosts that have little or no interest in the health and welfare of their guests, hosts that have little or no interest in adherence to community standards and regulations established for the welfare of the community at large, and hosts that commit tax fraud. And the list could go on.

Airbnb does have several value statements but, true to Chesky's comments, they don't have anything to do with integrity or honesty. And when apparent ethical failures are pointed out, at least until recently, the Airbnb official position has been, you guessed it, *"not our fault."* Guests are at fault if they stay at unsafe facilities. And hosts are at fault if they violate community ordinances and don't pay appropriate taxes, etc. *(I told you all the sins overlapped, didn't I?)*

Well, guess what? The *"disingenuous leadership"* part of Airbnb is now at a crossroads. Should they continue as the facilitator of the unethical practices and wait for the next crisis of scam listings, mass shootings, hidden cameras, unsafe facilities, community revolts, or legal actions?

Or should they accept the responsibility and fiduciary duty of ensuring that hosts operate ethically and legally with the guests *(customers)* interests as a priority? And should they adopt a formal, strong ethics value statement and begin the *"walk"* of conducting the business with integrity and honesty?

The good news is, as a result of several recent crises, Airbnb has announced plans to change its business model to a more ethical approach. But will the disingenuous leadership really go away? Will profits really get set aside for ethics? I'm going to say the same thing I did earlier about Facebook, *"we'll see."*

In 2019, the Business Roundtable (BRT), a nonprofit association whose members are CEOs of major U.S. companies, published a new *"Statement of the Purpose of a Corporation."* The Statement was well publicized because, for the first time, the BRT acknowledged the need for corporations to serve other stakeholders rather than the traditional primary focus on shareholders.

Well, I found it interesting that Alex Gorsky, the CEO of J&J and a board member of the BRT, was pictured on the cover of Fortune magazine as a spokesperson for the new Statement, on the eve of J&J being ordered to pay $465 million for its part in fueling the opioid crisis in Oklahoma. Seems to me J&J was going against the new Statement by putting shareholder profits above the safety of stakeholders (the patients). Just another case of *"disingenuous leadership."*

And then there is my favorite *"disingenuous leader,"* Theranos founder, Elizabeth Holmes. She would make a top ten list of disingenuous and unethical leaders of all time for her part in the now defunct *(and very disingenuous)* health technology company.

The company attracted investors after Holmes deceptively claimed the company had revolutionized blood testing by developing testing methods that could use surprisingly small volumes of blood. The company also had a distinguished group of board members who added credibility to the efforts; however, turned out to be a disingenuous *(or just plain duped)* group of individuals as well.

Holmes has been indicted on nine counts of wire fraud and two counts of conspiracy to commit wire fraud for *"distributing blood tests with falsified results to consumers."* This, after once being named *"the youngest and wealthiest self-made female billionaire in America"* with a $9 billion valuation *(Forbes,*

2015). Now, Holmes has a $0 net worth and thanks to Fortune magazine, she has made the list of the *"World's Most Disappointing Leaders."*

The bottom line – beware of organizations with leaders that talk about ethics *(yes, even Holmes touted Theranos' efforts as ethically "changing the world")* but do anything and everything but. Remember the *"talk"* can be very deceiving and effective in covering up unethical actions, but the *"walk"* is what stands at the end of the day. We will see if Airbnb stands, or falls like Theranos.

****

MOVE FAST AND BREAK THINGS

"...if everyone is told to think out of the box, you've got to expect that the boxes themselves will begin to deteriorate."
– Tina Brown

Facebook's co-founder and current CEO, Mark Zuckerberg, is quoted as saying *"Unless you are breaking stuff, you aren't moving fast enough."* The *"Move Fast and Break Things"* mentality was a motto at Facebook until 2014. But it seems to have continued to be a driving force at Facebook and applied generally and widely by many others, particularly high-tech, start-up companies *(yes, even Theranos – I know you are surprised there).* The goal is rapid growth at all costs with little or no regard for ethics and consequences.

The Facebook approach has been to launch products with little regard to the consequences of customers *(Facebook users)* and fix things *(after denials and deflection)* when an inevitable major crisis occurs. The attitude of Zuckerberg and Facebook is to blissfully move forward while *"breaking things"* in an attempt to change the world and rapidly grow the company. While Facebook is my prime example, they are far from alone in pursuing the *"break things"* strategy and mentality.

Google, Amazon, Microsoft, and Apple are all high-tech companies that have grown very rapidly, and they have the same ethical issues regarding personal privacy, data security, and information integrity, in general. And, the information technology issues are compounded due to the use of artificial intelligence (AI). The ethical issue with AI enters the picture via *"algorithmic bias,"* the systematic and repeatable errors in a computer system that create unfair outcomes. *That's a whole other issue to be discussed in Chapter 11.*

Let's just say, high-tech information-related companies have grown rapidly *(moved fast)* because they have developed the capability of gathering, storing, and selling huge amounts of data. They are also great at disseminating information whether it's the news *(biased or not)* or targeted marketing *(that's the AI part)* and advertisements *(misleading or not)*.

High-tech, in general, has *moved fast and broken things* by infringing on privacy, losing or non-transparently distributing *(think selling)* data, and communicating with a built-in AI driven bias.

Uber is another pretty good *"move fast and break things"* example. Uber, the ride sharing service, was founded in 2009 and since has grown to a company with over $18 billion in annual revenue (2019) and 3 million drivers globally. It was also on a list of the most disruptive companies in the world in 2018. *(Is this a good thing or a bad thing?)*

So, what's the *"break things"* part?

Aside from ongoing legal and regulatory issues, Uber reportedly tracks the location of Uber's customers, compromising consumer privacy. There are questions about the protocol for background checks of drivers in the interest of passenger welfare. And, multi-tasking drivers – Uber's selling point that nearby drivers are notified immediately – also raises safety concerns. Some also say Uber has a broken business model, which may be correct, given they lost $8.5 billion in 2019.

In Jonathan Taplin's book, *Move Fast and Break Things*, he describes the destruction of the traditional music industry by pirated music services, beginning with Napster. Napster is reported to have *"experienced the fastest growth of any digital service in history."* And in the process, the ethical business model of the music industry was broken. There were/are a wide range of methods people can share *(steal)* music via the web. All are representative of *"moving fast and breaking things,"* and much of it is illegal *(or at least, unethical)*.

Boeing was anxious to *"move fast"* and get past the implications of the two 737 Max planes crashes, proven by their failure to fully investigate the causes or their quick thought to hide the flawed flight control system. In the meantime, Boeing *"broke"* its reputation.

Genomics has far reaching potential for significant impact on medicine, saving lives, and society. Technology now allows for the editing of genes. The prospect is exciting for medical therapies *(think Coronavirus)* but has the potential for serious social harm. Applications require careful thought, addressing risks, and evaluating social impact. Not an area to *"move fast and break things."*

I like to show a video in my ethics trainings called "The Ethical Dilemma of Self-Driving Cars," after which I ask the question: *"Do you want 'move fast and break things' to be the mentality of the organizations developing self-driving cars?"* The answer: a resounding *"NO."*

We usually think of this issue only in terms of high-tech organizations. But remember the story about GardaWorld? The company is a literal example of *"moving fast and breaking things."* Garda was so intent on growing its business that it failed to invest in new equipment, truck repair, and maintenance. It also didn't take the time to train its drivers appropriately. The result – many equipment failures, traffic accidents, and sadly, deaths. A very sad example of *move fast and crash.*

So, is *move fast and break things* an ethical strategy? Likely not. No more than it is ethical to drive recklessly through a school zone, sell opioids on the street, or fly airplanes without the proper instruction.

So, the message here is: recklessness is not an ethical strategy, nor is moving so fast that serious, negative consequences are ignored. It doesn't make any difference whether the consequences are intentional or not, or whether the consequences are anticipated or unanticipated. Recklessness is wrong.

But, good news, many think that the *"move fast and break things"* era is just about over – although some haven't gotten the message yet. Make sure your organization has.

****

THE SMARTEST GUYS IN THE ROOM

> *"A man of genius is seldom ruined but by himself."*
> – Samuel Johnson

You may recognize *"The Smartest Guys in the Room"* phrase from a book and documentary film by the same name. It is a study of the Enron business scandal.

A common recipe for unethical conduct is executives with no integrity, total arrogance, limitless greed, and disregard for *all*, I mean *all stakeholders*. Remember the "Big Me" section. They mistakenly think they are the *"smartest guys in the room."* They believe they make all the rules whether they are legal or ethical or not.

They are usually oblivious of consequences *(if I make the rules, then there can't be any adverse consequences)* and/or any thought they were doing something wrong. They drive the organization for personal gain and see the stakeholders as a means to achieve their personal objectives. In their view the stakeholders work for the executive, not the other way around. Much more about shareholders and stakeholders to follow.

Remember the poster executive for this behavior – former Tyco CEO, Dennis Kozlowski – quoted as saying *"you become consumed... by your own arrogance and you really think that you can do anything."*

Other examples are former WorldCom executives – CFO Scott Sullivan and CEO Bernard Ebbers, former Adelphia CEO John Rigas, and the Enron crew of former Chairman and CEO Kenneth Lay, former CEO Jeffrey Skilling, and former CFO Andy Fastow. I'm sure you know the stories, but if not, check them out.

> *"The sad fact is that it takes just a handful of employees to destroy a company of many thousand innocent individuals."*
> – Biegelman and Bartow

The *"Smartest Guys in the Room"* set the bar low for ethical conduct. Then others see it and often copy the behavior. The next thing you know, there is an organization full of *"the smartest guys"* that think that they can do anything together. The *"smart guys"* think of loopholes and shortcuts, use financial engineering to achieve goals, and see complexity as a tool to obscure the facts and truth. They brainstorm ways of inflating revenue, earnings, and profits while understating liabilities and losses. And, of course, hiding relevant information from customers, investors, analysts, and regulators goes with the territory.

The *"smart guys"* also have no problem with self-dealings including bribes, kickbacks, conflicts of interest, insider trading, and individual tax violations for personal gain. And, finally, the *"smart guys"* are perfectly capable of obstruction of justice, perjury, witness tampering, or other obstructive behavior when they are in a bind.

But just remember, ironically, these *"smart guys"* are the not so smart for the organization in the end.

****

THE LAWYERS AND AUDITORS APPROVED IT

One of the primary arguments of Enron executives for their behavior was that the attorneys and auditors approved the schemes.

> *Just because an attorney and/or an auditor says it's legal,*
> *doesn't automatically make it ethical.*

Most external auditors are professional and adhere to the standards of independence and competence but a few *(well publicized)* auditors can't separate the fact that they are paid by the client and, therefore, compromise their independent judgment. They become conflicted and look for loopholes on behalf of the client who is paying for their work. They sometimes cross the line and put the illegitimate interests *(and means)* of the client before the interests of the shareholders and public *(all other stakeholders),* the parties whose interests' auditors are supposed to protect.

Lawyers are simply hired to look out for the client's interests. Period. No other stakeholders. Further, they are focused on the law, not ethics. It may be legal, but is it right? Most lawyers are of little help and may unintentionally set an ethics trap. *"The attorney said it was legal, so I did it."* An ethical decision is most likely legal, but just because something is legal doesn't mean it meets the ethics test. *(See the Ethical Anchors chapter.)* Sissela Bok describes some attorneys as master manipulators of the truth on behalf of their clients, a pretty accurate description.

Eugene Soltes starts one of the chapters in his book, *Why They Do It,* by asking the question. If there was no legal prohibition against murder, would you kill someone? Would your friends and associates? Would everyone?

As most know, Enron was one of the worst specific cases of auditor and attorney professional failure. A Big Six (at the time there were six) public accounting firm, Arthur Anderson, proved that some auditors cannot be trusted to give good advice. The auditors were inherently conflicted by the business relationship. And, external auditors don't generally look for or find fraud anyway. So, don't hide behind the fact there was auditor approval. It doesn't mean much. *(Sorry, harsh, I know – but I speak the truth.)*

Likewise, the Enron case is an example of professional failure of an organization's lawyers. Lawyers are also inherently conflicted by the business relationship. Outside lawyers were hired in the Enron case to investigate potential irregularities regarding Enron's crucial partnership relationships. The lawyers blessed the arrangements just days before the beginning of Enron's collapse. Not a good idea to hide behind your attorney either.

The point is, some organizations will engage in serious illegal acts, particularly when an attorney or auditor finds a loophole and blesses *(or does not object to)* the behavior and actions.

After hiding behind the auditor/lawyer shield for quite a while in legal proceedings, Enron's CFO finally admitted that, even though his actions at the time were determined by Enron legal and audit staff to be legal, he knew they were wrong.

Just because an organization can, doesn't necessarily make it right.

****

EVERYONE DOES IT, SO IT MUST BE OK

Let's face it, the financial services industry is known for deception. Advertising material states that the *"customer comes first"* or *"we do better when our clients do better"* – as one TV ad claims. But in practice, many in the industry recommend products to customers that provide the greatest commissions, rather than offer comparable products with lower fees. Studies conducted by Bogle's Investment Research firm show that the pushing of fee products costs investors 1% annually of their investment.

So, why is it done? Partly because it is in the self-interest of the investment representative, but also, because *"everyone does it."* And trust me – even if everyone isn't doing it, enough of them are, so it still doesn't seem wrong.

It's not just financial services. There are many examples where actions are not consistent with stated company values or codes of conduct simply because "everyone does it" or "that's the way it's always been done."

As mentioned previously, GardaWorld has wonderful value statements and standards of conduct on its website. But, on the job and in the field, the picture is quite different. Although some complained, it appears many others went along with *(and still are going along with)* the poor maintenance and unsafe practices, perhaps because that was/is normal practice at Garda. *"Everyone (at least at Garda) does it that way."* Oh, and when the Director of Risk Management brought this to senior management's attention, she was terminated – which reinforced that change was not about to happen. Sadly, the *"everyone does it"* mentality will win every time against organization value statements or codes of conduct, when they conflict.

The entire subject of financial engineering is an *"everyone does it"* mentality. From the legendary accounting practices that enabled General Electric (GE), under Jack Welch's reign, to deliver stable earnings quarter after quarter, to all those who copied GE over the years, the practices that *"everyone does"* no doubt – even post-Sarbanes Oxley regulations – live on.

The book by Howard Schilit, *Financial Shenanigans*, details the many techniques that enable companies to dupe their investors, ranging from fudging estimates and projections to out and out fraud. Some practices that are border line get pushed over the edge with legal and audit approval. *(Overlap of sins, yet again.)* Others are adopted because of an organization's financial pressures, self-interest, pressure from the boss, known weak internal controls, and/or lack of external oversight. All are often fueled by the impression *(real or imagined)* that *everyone does it.*

The pharmaceutical and medical equipment industries are legionary for their sales and marketing tactics. The details will be reviewed in more detail in a subsequent section of Chapter Eight on *"favors, gifts, bribes, and kickbacks."* But the approach can be summarized as one that always serves the supplier and sales representatives' financial interests, sometimes at the expense of the patients' interest.

The sales process is full of these tactics to influence the physicians' decisions to prescribe the products represented. The tactics are common in the industry. The opioid crisis has been fueled by such behavior. And it must be okay, because *everyone is doing it.* At least that seems to be the mentality of industry insiders that are okay with the misleading marketing campaigns and false advertising.

> *"Money can extinguish intrinsic motivation, diminish performance, crush creativity, encourage unethical behavior, foster short-term thinking, and become addictive."*
> – Daniel H. Pink

The sad part is that there are always some who comply with not only the letter but the spirit and intent of laws, regulations, values, codes, etc. without hesitation. But, as Soltes states, *"Sustaining... in the face of competing pressures can be difficult."* Why? Because *"everybody does it."* And it can be lucrative.

If an organization is relying on an ethics test of *"everyone's doing it,"* think again and look around, because everyone isn't. And on a more positive note, if everyone is doing the right thing, that rubs off too. That will be one of the themes of the remaining organizational ethics chapters.

****

EVERYTHING IS GREY

"Grey is not a substitute for black and white."
– Jon M. Huntsman

You are the purchasing manager for your organization. A vendor sales representative has a vacation condo next to a golf course on Hilton Head Island. The rep knows you are a golfer. There is a standing offer for free use of the condo whenever you want. You have checked the code of conduct for your organization and it doesn't say you can't. *It's a "grey" area. What do you do?*

Your company has just acquired a small business located in Southern California. You are the Head of Human Resources (HR) with the acquiring company. On your first trip to the plant, the local HR Manager tells you that many of the employees are illegal immigrants with falsified documentation. Your attorney tells you there is no problem because there is no legal requirement to further check into the status of the employees. It would be very costly to replace the employees and the owner of your business has no interest in spending the money. *It's a grey area. What do you do?*

You are the CFO of a privately-owned company financed through bonds. In a conference call with bond holders, the President of your company paints a much rosier picture of your business forecast than actually exists. In fact, the President is indicating sales forecasts are up when, at the same time, you are making plans for shutting down some operations due to a lack of orders. Other executives are on the call and they know the real truth. Maybe, things will pick up soon. Who really knows? No need to worry the investors. *It's a grey area. What do you do?*

Your company, U.S. based, has recently purchased a company in Canada. They are in the same manufacturing business with very similar processes. On first look, the Canadian operation seems to rarely have machine guards and they ignore other safety practices that you are used to. When questioned, the local plant manager explains that things are *different* in Canada regarding safety and, in fact, he has a great relationship with the local safety inspector. He says, all is fine although you are not so sure. *It's a grey area. What do you do?*

To the players in the 2008 financial crisis, it was all a *grey area.* In no particular order, but let's start with the rating agencies. Rating agencies classified subprime securities as investment grade. It may have been incompetence or because there was a conflict of interest. *Or, just because it was a grey area.*

Then there were the bank regulators. It could have been the infighting among the agencies but the effect was to insufficiently examine savings and investment banks leading up to the crisis. *Or, maybe it was just a grey area.*

On to the mortgage bank processes. Banks had traditionally retained most loans that they originated, which provided a built-in incentive to make sure they were good loans with a small chance of default. Securitization of loans led to a drop in underwriting standards. *In any event, the standards became a grey area.*

Naturally, fancy financial instruments were developed that allowed institutional investors of the securities to ensure against loan defaults. But, no one truly knew the underlying quality of the loans of the instruments that were being insured. *It was a very grey area.*

Then there were homeowners who wanted to get rich quick by flipping houses and a little fudging on loan applications became routine. And because the mortgage companies wanted to get rich quick by increasing loan volumes, and the appraisers wanted to get rich quick by increasing their volumes – the documentation supporting the ability of the homeowner to repay the loan and the underlying value of the appraised property *all became grey areas.*

The real world is made up of lots of grey area, right?

You can always deny and deflect. Or, make some disingenuous comments about ethics and do the opposite. Better yet, just say you were so busy moving fast that a few things slipped. Besides, you're smart and make good calls all the time. People admire you for your ingenuity. Anyhow, the lawyers and auditors signed off and everyone else does it too. And, *it's all a grey area anyway.*

Or is it? The Everyday Ethicist agrees with Huntsman:

> *"Grey is not a substitute for black and white."*
> – Jon M. Huntsman

It's black and white.

Don't fall prey to the Seven Deadly Sins of *(Unethical)* Organizations.

****

AN (UN)ETHICAL WORK ENVIRONMENT

Many factors contribute to an unhealthy work environment that increases the risk of unethical conduct. As mentioned already, the often-cited factors begin with the *"tone at the top"* – leaders that don't seem to care about ethics and who do not *"walk the ethics talk."* I mean, if they don't care, why should I?

Other factors include a lack of recognition for job performance. The employee attitude is, if I am not recognized for my contributions, why should I care about the company? Employees who perceive inequities in compensation may attempt to make up the difference through unethical means rationalizing that the end *(fair compensation)* justifies the means *(stealing)*.

Autocratic rather than participative and collaborative organizations can also create an unethical environment. Autocratic leaders don't like *"bad news"* so subordinates give them what they want even though it may not be the truth.

Employees may resent the autocratic nature of leaders and look for ways to compensate themselves and/or *"pay back"* the company for their stress/resentment. Also, autocratic leaders can simply direct unethical conduct and due to the culture the organization seemingly supports, the order will go unquestioned.

Here's a recently uncovered *(2020)* example. The controlling, autocratic CEO of the Florida Coalition Against Domestic Violence directed the CFO and Chief Operating Officer to pay her millions of additional year-end compensation *(diverting grant funds intended for victim services)*. Although the subordinates believed the payments were excessive and unethical, they claimed a defense that they were just following orders.

Low morale *(for a variety of reasons)* may also lead to a rise in unethical conduct. Unreasonable expectations without reasonable resources can lead to *"cutting corners"* that turn out to be unethical. Directing activities without appropriate training can lead to *"shortcuts"* that amount to unethical conduct. Disregard for the health and welfare of employees can fuel retaliatory conduct that may be unethical.

The justifications and rationalizations of organization unethical conduct are endless. But if we each take the time to understand it, work to improve it, and guard against the organizational sins, we can pave the road to becoming an Everyday Ethical Organization.

THIS IS THE (UN)ETHICAL ORGANIZATION PROPOSITION.

Now that we've traveled the road (and seen some potholes), it's time to journey into the details of what makes an Everyday Ethical Organization. From stakeholders and priorities... values, standards, and conduct... to processes that support ethical conduct.

YOUR (UN)ETHICAL ORGANIZATION CHOICES

Do leaders (and employees in general) tend to deny responsebility when things go wrong?

Do leaders (and employees in general) tend to deflect and blame others when things go wrong?

Are leaders disingenuous when directing activities that they know are wrong while trumpeting corporate values to the contrary?

Is there a "grow the numbers at all cost" mentality?

Are leaders' expectations for growth reasonable or unreasonable with the resources provided?

Is innovation done with such speed that there is little time for thoughtful reflection on the impact of others?

Is the organization led by the "smartest guys in the room" who think they have answers for everything and who solicit very little input and collaboration?

Do leaders hide behind lawyers' and auditors' opinions when engaged in questionable activity?

Is there a "I know it is wrong, but everyone's doing it" mentality present at the organization?

Are ethical issues generally considered "grey areas" and open for interpretation?

Is there an unhealthy work environment that increases the risk of unethical conduct?

CHAPTER SEVEN:

ETHICAL ORGANIZATIONS

(STAKEHOLDERS AND PRIORITIES)

AS PREVIOUSLY MENTIONED, A 2018 Gallup Poll of Americans' confidence in U.S. institutions showed that small businesses are among the highest rated. Only the military was rated higher. Big business, on the other hand, was rated as one of the worst *(along with congress, television news, and the criminal justice system)*. Polls show that more are dissatisfied with big business than are satisfied.

So, why are small businesses respected more than large businesses? I suggest it has to do with their approach to stakeholders. That's you and me – who are employees, contractors, customers, vendors, shareholders, investors, or members of the community or society at large. Stakeholders are anyone who comes into contact with an institution in *any* way. Those who have a *"stake"* in the activities of the organization.

When you think of big business, what do you think of *(besides being dissatisfied, as we noted above already)?* According to the Reputational Institute *(I mean, who better to ask),* many think of lack of social responsibility, poor workplace environment, and poor leadership. Social responsibility has to do with honesty, transparency, and credibility. Work environment has to do with empathy, caring, and just plain being human. Leadership has to do with integrity and values. All pretty much add up to ethics – *or in the case of big business* – the lack thereof.

When I think about small businesses, which the data shows we are most satisfied with, I think of the chapter in my *Choices* book on *Choosing an Ownership and Entrepreneurship Mindset.* I list many qualities that I think are important to running a business; however, I believe the most important of these is trust. When a small business does it right, when they listen to needs and are close to all their stakeholders – their communities, employees, and customers to name a few – they build trust. *(Think about Truett Cathy's view when Chick-fil-A was small and even now after it has grown.)*

Whether a big or small business, the path to becoming an Everyday Ethical Organization begins by building trust through utilizing the right stakeholder model and thoughtfully considering stakeholder priorities.

"Exceptional businesses sustain bottom-line results, which they invest to create meaningful, positive impact for their stakeholders."
– Punit Renjen

In 2005, John C. Bogle wrote and published the book *The Battle for the Soul of Capitalism*. The subtitle of the book is *"How the financial system undermined social ideals, damaged trust in the markets, robbed investors of trillions – and what to do about it."* Although the book was written in the context of the investment business, its meaning and message applies widely for all organizations.

Bogle's main point is that when organizations and institutions get to the point where stakeholders *(one or more)* do not trust them, they have lost their *"soul"* and *"damaged trust."* Bogle wrote, *"Only capitalists can kill capitalism."* In this book, I'll say *"only (unethical) leaders can kill their organizations."*

Global investment management firm, BlackRock, Inc.'s CEO, Larry Fink, seems to have gotten Bogle's message, as he announced in a 2020 letter to investors the company's position to factor in environmental and social issues into investment decisions. Both Bogle and Fink have been outspoken advocates of consideration of all stakeholder interests in investing.

As previously mentioned, in 2019 the BRT issued a new *"Statement on the Purpose of a Corporation,"* which includes the following key points for commitment:

o   Delivering value to customers;

o   Investing in employees;

o   Dealing fairly and ethically with suppliers;

o   Supporting communities; and

o   Generating long-term value to shareholders.

The Statement concluded by saying, *"Each of our stakeholders is essential."* The significance of the new statement is that it represented a move away from a primary focus on shareholders, and now includes a commitment to *all* stakeholders.

But, what does the change really mean? It means that they finally acknowledge that stakeholders *(other than shareholders)* need to be able to trust corporations to do the right thing. *It is all about trust and ethics.*

In recent years, a lot has been written about venture capital firms and shareholder versus stakeholder approaches to business. Maybe the contrast is most stark in a venture capital environment. A venture capital firm invests in a business to obtain a return on investment for the firm managers and those who invest in their firm. Collectively, all could be labeled as shareholders and the mission is clear: *make money.*

But then there are those pesky other stakeholders – employees, suppliers, communities, etc. How do we treat them when it is not so clear how they will affect the ability to *"make money?"* Once again, it is all about organizational ethics, whether a big company or small, venture capital or not.

In 2019, the Rock Center for Corporate Governance at Stanford University surveyed 209 company CEOs and CFOs to *"understand the role that stakeholder interests play in long-term corporate planning."* The results indicate a mix of outlooks with executives divided over whether stakeholder initiatives *(other than shareholders)* are a cost or a benefit to the company.

To me, this is a pretty scary result from an ethical standpoint but truly explains the unethical actions of leaders described at the beginning of *The Everyday Ethical Leader* chapter and the various rationales described in the *(Un)Ethical Organization* chapter.

Either organizations are only looking out for shareholders, sometimes at the expense of others... or they look out for all stakeholders' interests, every time, all the time. The latter, of course, is The Everyday Ethical Organization approach. Again, just think of the organizations of Cathy, Huntsman, and Bogle for starters.

But, by now you know in order to find the right ethical path, we have to examine the wrong one – in this case – the existing business models. Sorry, you have to take the negative before we get to the positive... again. I don't think there is a better way to prove my point.

SHAREHOLDERS ARE PRIMARY

The *shareholders are primary* view *(ascribed to by the famed economist, Milton Friedman)* is that the sole responsibility of an enterprise is to make a profit for its investors. Friedman argued that responsibilities to all other stakeholders are secondary.

The *shareholders are primary* argument goes like this: with no financing, there is usually no business, so, let's take care of the shareholders even if we have to cut corners when it comes to the interests of others who have a stake in the business. Many companies *(whether they admit publicly or not)* have this mindset and method of operation.

The existence of this mindset is supported by the BRT's new statement that in effect acknowledges a need to *change* the mission of the corporation to more broadly serve all stakeholders. Although some responsible companies, large and small, have been operating with a balanced stakeholder approach forever, to me the new statement clearly acknowledges that many have not and are not.

A lot of today's business organizations still operate in principle and practice with shareholders' *(banks, bond holders, individual stock and equity mutual fund investors, and private equity investors)* interests primary. Executives' compensation depends on hitting the numbers, meeting or exceeding analysts' projections, and/or anything that will increase the value of shareholder holdings. Executive compensation is also heavily weighted on share price through stock options.

When things go wrong ethically, sometimes overtly but usually quietly, organizations deflect blame of unethical behavior on the basis that the actions were taken for the benefit of shareholders. The attitude is: *"What was I supposed to do, go out of business?"* A difficult situation perhaps, but still no excuse for unethical conduct.

In my opinion, the leaders of the *shareholders are primary* organizations are guilty of creating a culture not much different than a Ponzi scheme – paying *"recent"* investors with the lives and livelihood of others, compromising or ignoring the interests of employees, customers, suppliers, and communities *("earlier" investors)*.

VW ran a Ponzi scheme of this variety, deceiving customers and violating environment regulations in order to increase market share and achieve other financial objectives for *the benefit of the shareholders.*

BP sacrificed the health and safety of oil platform workers and the gulf ocean and surrounding environment in order to increase oil production and improve financial performance for *the benefit of the shareholders.*

J&J, Purdue Pharma, and others in the pharmaceutical industry ignored the welfare of its customers and patients in order to drive opioid sales up and increase revenue for *the benefit of the shareholders.*

Other organizations mentioned in this book to one degree or another sacrificed other legitimate stakeholder interests in favor of shareholders: Boeing, Airbnb, Facebook, Uber, Enron, just to name a few.

Does Boeing really think that travelers' lives are less important than profits? Does BP really think employees' safety is less important than operating output? Does J&J really think that patient health is less important than sales growth? Publicly, most corporations will say that all stakeholders' interests are valued equally but do they *really* mean it? Actions speak louder than words. *What you do is who you are.*

****

THE SHAREHOLDER, EMPLOYEES, AND CUSTOMERS ARE PRIMARY APPROACH

In the process of conducting research for this book, I read the recently *(2019)* published textbook *Business Ethics* written by K. Praveen Parbotteeah and John B. Cullen. *(Great comprehensive book on business ethics which I highly recommend.)*

The authors state that their preferences are for an all stakeholder approach to business ethics. However, when it came to the discussion of stakeholders, the authors went out of their way to frame business ethics in terms of *"primary"* stakeholders and *"secondary"* stakeholders. Primary stakeholders were defined as shareholders *(suppliers of equity capital)*, customers, and employees. Secondary stakeholders are defined as governments as regulative institutions, non-governmental organizations (NGOs) who represent special interests, and the media *(the primary keeper of reputations)*.

At best, framing an organization's stakeholders as *primary* or *secondary* is arbitrary; at worst, it is the mindset that is at the root of an organization's unethical conduct. I mean, let's think about it. Is making money for shareholders more important than lives? Is making money for shareholders more important than the reputation of an organization? Is making money for shareholders more important than obeying the law? Unethical organizations think so.

When organizations think in terms of primary and secondary stakeholders, their ethical troubles truly begin. One chapter in *Business Ethics* begins with the Nike example of managing suppliers and issues regarding working conditions. Nike saw suppliers as secondary stakeholders – it's not our problem what they do – they are *"secondary"* when it comes to our ethics priorities. Well, times have changed, and Nike is now proactively managing ethical issues of its suppliers. And I bet Nike would say they are every bit as important as shareholders, employees, and customers.

****

I know, I know – I am beginning to sound like a broken record. But to sum up the negatives of the *"primary... anyone"* approach, let's recap:

BP learned quickly that increasing oil rig output at the expense of employee safety and environmental protection was a mistake.

VW learned that increasing market share and being the number one manufacturer of vehicles at the expense of customer fraud and violation of regulations was a mistake.

Wells Fargo learned that achieving internal, organizational performance goals of increased customer accounts at the expense of their reputation and customer trust was a mistake.

And while Facebook still seems to think that revenue growth and profit is more important than data security and privacy of its users and *"fake news"* distribution to the public, they too will learn this is a mistake.

I believe there is no such thing as a secondary stakeholder. Organizations and their leaders should work for all stakeholders.

****

VALUE ALL STAKEHOLDERS

The *Value All Stakeholders* approach obviously acknowledges the need to make decisions that meet the balanced best interests of all stakeholders *(the point that the BRT now seems to be embracing)*. So, who exactly are the stakeholders in a business or organization? And what are their *(sometimes competing and conflicting)* priorities and concerns?

Shareholders – Those who own stock in a company or who otherwise receive benefits from investments in a company.

Profitability of the organization

Financial sustainability (Going concern)
Market share
Integrity of financials
Transparency of communications
Executive compensation and incentives
Board oversight
Corporate governance and controls
Leadership integrity

<u>Customers</u> – Those who buy goods or services from a business.

Price fairness and transparency
Honest advertising
Marketing incentives
Honest and transparent communications
Customer complaint processes
Customer data security and privacy

<u>Employees</u> – Those who are hired to perform services for a company.

Code of conduct establishment, administration, enforcement
Health and safety policies
Ethics policy and whistleblower protections
Compensation equity and incentive plans
Honest and transparent communications
Leadership integrity and respect
Performance monitoring and job security
Financial sustainability (Going concern)

<u>Suppliers, Vendors, and Contractors</u> – Those who sell goods or services to an organization.

Contract administration integrity
Honest and transparent communications

Favors, Bribes, Gifts, Kickbacks
Contractor health and safety

<u>NGOs</u> – <u>N</u>on-<u>G</u>overnmental <u>O</u>rganizations are independent of any government but may set professional standards of conduct that are of common interest to a stakeholder group.

Professional codes of conduct compliance
Lobbying efforts

<u>Media</u> – This category is intended to include all who impact the reputation of the organization.

Honest and complete communications
Transparency of communications

<u>Governments and Communities</u> – Society that is impacted by the decisions of organizations.

Respecting laws and regulations in spirit and intent
Transparency of communications
Environmental issues
Community support
Corporate responsibility
Corporate fiduciary responsibility

And last but not least, I'll add an eighth class of stakeholders.

<u>Friends and Families</u> – Those family members and close friends of those associated with the organization – maybe the most important stakeholder of all!

Work/life balance
Income and job security
Health and safety
Community support
Corporate responsibility

As you can see, there are a lot of stakeholders and even more potential areas for conflict when it comes to priorities and/or concerns. *(And keep in mind, the list is representative but by no means all inclusive.)*

The first step in becoming an ethical organization is to recognize all stakeholders on your list and deal openly and honestly with potential conflicts in priorities among the stakeholder groups.

The second step is to create a unique ethical mindset, one that perhaps inverts the traditional stakeholder list of importance *(by the way, I presented the traditional order above, with shareholders coming first).* Here's my out-of-the-box *(I know, I hate that phrase too)* innovative thinking about organization ethics. I'll call it the...

****

INVERTED STAKEHOLDER PYRAMID

I created this inverted stakeholder pyramid mindset from the business approach of my step great-grandfather, Archie Peck. I'll share a little background on Archie to help set the stage.

Archie was briefly mentioned in the introduction of this book but also made an appearance in my *Choices* book. He was recognized in the chapter, *Choosing Development.* The point of the chapter is to highlight the choices people make that contribute to their personal or professional effectiveness. Personally, Archie was a WWI recipient of the Medal of Honor for his extraordinary bravery, risking his life to save others. However, professionally, after the war, Archie returned home to Western New York to start his career in the food distribution industry and later start and run his own business while raising five boys *(one of whom was my step grandfather)*.

A. A. PECK & SONS GENERAL STORE

So, what did Archie's stakeholder pyramid look like?

First and foremost, Archie emphasized taking care of his family's financial and emotional needs and leaving a legacy of a business for his sons to grow and expand over the years. *The primary stakeholder and the largest piece (top) of the inverted pyramid – Care for family.*

Next, Archie was a morally sound, kind, community service-oriented person who knew that following the rules and obeying the law was essential for good citizenship and a solid business reputation. He learned that as a child and I'm sure it was reinforced in the military. And, he instinctively knew that good citizens naturally attracted customers; people want to buy things from people they trust. *Next on the pyramid – Ensure good citizenship and community service.*

"In a free enterprise, the community is not just another stakeholder in business, but is in fact, the very purpose of its existence."
– Jamsetji Tata

Archie spent his career in the grocery business and learned the business from a leading grocery chain of the era. He learned the regulations of the industry and professional standards of managing a food distribution and retail business. He was proud of his profession and knew that high standards attracted customers. *Next on the pyramid – Maintain professional standards.*

Then, Archie knew that based on his knowledge of the industry, his reputation in the community, and his organic ability to attract customers that suppliers *(of produce and dry goods)* would look forward to supplying the needs of his business. Archie always treated suppliers and vendors with respect, because after all, without his suppliers, there was no product to sell to customers! *Next on the pyramid – Respect your suppliers and vendors.*

As the business grew, there was a need to add additional employees outside of the family, and you guessed it, every kid in town wanted to work for *"Archie at the General Store."* There were plenty of family members, friends, and neighbors whose first job was at Archie's store. *(One of whom was my stepmother; she loves to tell stories about being the egg sorter!)* They wanted to work there because they knew they would be treated with kindness, compensated fairly, and treated as they were Archie's extended family. *Next on the pyramid – Value your employees.*

So, Archie had already set the stage for his business – with a strong family focus, being a good community steward and a law-abiding citizen, a true professional in his industry, who takes care of vendors, suppliers, and employees. There wasn't much else needed to attract customers. But you can bet Archie knew every customer that walked through the door. *Next on the pyramid – Take care of customers.*

And, finally, Archie knew that if he respected the needs of his family *(near and long-term),* served his community honorably, maintained high professional standards in the conduct of his business, partnered with his suppliers to add good value to his customers, attracted and retained good service oriented employees, the local bank would race to finance Archie's capital needs over the years. *The local bank (the shareholder in this case) wanted to invest in Archie because he took care of ALL his stakeholders. Note, this is the smallest piece (bottom) of the inverted pyramid, as it should be.*

We just inverted the traditional stakeholder pyramid!

(And now you know why there was a random pyramid pictured on the first page of this chapter. ☺)

Creating an ethical organization is to establish a mindset of priorities as follows:

Family Values
Laws & Regulations
Reputation of Trust and Community-Focus
High Professional Standards
Quality Supplier Partnerships
Dedicated, Customer-Oriented Employees
Value to Customers
Shareholder Commitments

****

The rest of the story: Because of his effective implementation *(unknowingly to him)* of the inverted stakeholder pyramid mindset, one of Archie's sons *(my step grandfather)* took over the General Store and continued Archie's legacy of running an ethical, successful business. The other sons founded and ran successful grocery businesses as well.

"Operate businesses and organizations as if they're family owned."
– Jon M. Huntsman

As a final side note, Andy Fastow, the former Enron CFO who was convicted for his role in the financial fraud, has said that if those at Enron had made decisions as if they were leaving the business to their children, it would have eliminated most *(if not all)* of their unethical actions.

Family first organizations invert the traditional stakeholder pyramid. *Shareholder* first organizations... well, they can really screw things up. It's no accident that our initial statistics show small businesses as highly rated. They keep their priorities in order and respect the interests of *all* stakeholders.

THIS IS THE ETHICAL ORGANIZATION STAKEHOLDER AND PRIORITIES PROPOSITION.

Now on to values, standards, and conduct at The Everyday Ethical Organization...

Explore Your Ethical Organization
Stakeholders and Priorities

What would be the public confidence rating of your organization?

Why do large organizations tend to rate low in public confidence?

Why do small organizations tend to rate high in public confidence?

What role does trust play in the success of an organization?

Who are the stakeholders to your organization?

Does your organization put shareholders' interests first, ahead of other stakeholders?

What are the pitfalls of the "shareholders are primary" approach? Describe ethical problems that you have seen as a result of this approach.

What are the potential conflicts in priorities with other stakeholders of the "shareholders are primary" approach?

Do you believe it is possible for an organization to be successful balancing the competing interests and priorities of all stakeholders?

Does your organization value all stakeholders? How could you help them identify ways to better prioritize stakeholders and/or stakeholder priorities? (Think inverted pyramid.)

CHAPTER EIGHT:

ETHICAL ORGANIZATIONS
(VALUES, STANDARDS, ENFORCEMENT)

WE LEARNED IN THE *Ethical Mirage* chapter that ethical conduct cannot be taken for granted. We are not as ethical as we think we are – no question about it. It has been proven through many studies over many years. There are too many unknown variables when dealing with people of varied backgrounds, experiences, values, and beliefs to predict behavior. Airbnb's CEO's view of the world – that we all inherently have integrity and honestly as values in our lives and we need not explicitly state those values to deter unethical conduct – is just dead wrong.

Furthermore, according to deception researcher Timothy Levine, human beings are terrible at deception detection. See

Levine's book, *Duped: Truth Default Theory,* for a very detailed analysis with plenty of supporting evidence of why we fail at deception detection.

So even if we are not counting on ethical conduct all the time, we are not going to be bailed out by our abilities to detect unethical conduct when it occurs.

> *The conclusion:*
>
> *We can't assume that human beings will behave ethically, and we can't even trust our instincts to detect those who don't behave ethically.*

So, how on earth can we assure that people in our organizations will act ethically? Take it from Levine, the only answer is *deterrence.*

> *"...the human solution to the problem of deception is deterrence."*
> – Timothy R. Levine

In other words, in order for organizations to ensure ethical conduct, there needs to be a serious effort to promote ethical conduct and to deter and prevent unethical conduct. It simply can't be taken for granted. And remember, if you buy David Brooks' logic *(The Road to Character),* our ethics is trending toward worse, not better. So, we need this now, more than ever.

****

Remember the data that indicated that the public has a lot of confidence in small businesses and the military? I suspect the reason that the military is highly rated may be partly due to patriotism, but mostly due to the fact that there are consistent values and standards of conduct in all branches and levels of the military. And the consistent values and standards are not just there in *"talk,"* they are consistently reinforced with training and are uniformly enforced. *(Anyone who knows anything about the military knows they walk the talk.)*

People respect the fact that there are clear values and standards in the military and the military leaders know it results in a more effective organization. And in case you are wondering, the U.S. Army values are: *Loyalty, Duty, Respect, Selfless Service, Honor, Integrity, and Personal Courage (LDRSHIP).* Awesome, if you ask me *(and who doesn't love a good acronym).* There are some big companies out there that should take note.

****

So, why does the general public have so much confidence in small businesses? As outlined in the last chapter, I believe it is because small businesses generally operate in the spirit of individual's with strong values, like the Archie Peck, John C. Bogle, or Truett Cathy's of the world.

For small businesses to survive, they need to build trust – with bankers, suppliers, employees, customers, and the communities in which they operate. As I state in my *Choices* book, *"people buy things and engage services from people they trust."* And, *"people are trusted because they have a record of honesty, integrity, character, and fair play."* Small businesses don't stay in business very long if they don't meet their commitments and always do the right things. They have to have trusting relationships in order to survive.

****

The goal of every organization should be to create a ripple effect *(yes, again, the reason for the picture at the beginning of the chapter)* of ethical choices and ethical decision making. No more Big Me's, Ethical Rationalizers, or Disingenuous Leaders. The objective is to build an Everyday Ethical Organization full of ethical people making ethical decisions every day.

The remainder of this chapter will lay out a plan to build an ethical organization that is as respected as small businesses and the military seem to be. If you believe your organization is already highly ethical, the following should serve as a checklist to keep it that way.

The Everyday Ethical Organization framework is all about:

VALUES

STANDARDS

ENFORCEMENT

ORGANIZATION VALUES: INCLUDING ETHICS

Blanchard and Peale, in their book *The Power of Ethical Management,* observe that companies *"speak eloquently about values of honesty, integrity, and sincerity – but the company... consists of misrepresentations, exaggerations, and sometimes outright lies."*

I have talked a lot already throughout the book about *"walking the talk."* The implication is if there is no action or follow through, the talk is meaningless, particularly in the ethics realm. Horowitz made the point by the phrase, *"what you do is who you are."* He didn't say, *"you are who you say you are."* In a previous chapter, I talked about characteristics of unethical organizations including disingenuous leaders – those that are all talk about ethics with little action to back it up.

So, you might conclude that there is really no reason to even do the *talk* about ethics. Just do whatever you are going to do and hope it is ethical. Let your actions *(your walk)* be the whole story. But, there is a fallacy in this logic. So, let's get this part out of the way at the beginning. *Value statements and other communications about ethics do count.*

Remember professor and psychologist, Dan Ariely? To determine whether reminders and awareness make any difference in influencing ethical conduct, Ariely set up a very simple study. He took a group of 450 students and split them into two groups. Half were asked to remember the Ten Commandments; the other half were asked to recall ten books they had read recently. Both groups were then assigned to complete a test, which had a built-in opportunity to cheat.

Among the group who had to recall the books, there was a normal amount of cheating *(benchmarked through previous studies)*. Among the Ten Commandments group, there was no cheating. Yes, *no* cheating.

Others have done similar behavioral research and come up with similar results. In general, the studies indicate that making values visible is a good personal reminder of expected conduct. *Reminders and awareness of values does count.*

> *"Recalling moral standards at the time of temptation can work wonders to decrease [unethical] behavior and potentially prevent it altogether."*
> – Dan Ariely

The *"working wonders"* may be a little strong but highly ethical organizations are firm believers in establishing, communicating, and reinforcing organization ethical values.

No Ethical Value Statements

But, before we get further into the importance of ethical value statements, let's look at the *"No Ethical Value Statements"* universe. Yes, same note as before applies – the negatives always help drive home the point – so you have to stick with me through them again.

Facebook has chosen to have value statements that say nothing about honesty, trust, integrity, or character. *Be Bold, Focus on Impact, Move Fast (are we surprised here?), Be Open, Build Social Value* are what exists today. Not one inkling of doing things ethically. Even openness is meaningless if you aren't adding "honest" to it. Is it a wonder Facebook has a beleaguered reputation?

Let's pick on Airbnb again, too. Their core values include: *Champion the Mission, Be a Host, Simplify, Every Frame Matters, Be a Cereal Entrepreneur, and Embrace the Adventure.* There may be a little ethics tucked in there somewhere, but it is not readily apparent *(and not likely given CEO Chesky's previous speeches/stance).* I have already described some serious ethical issues at Airbnb these days; do you think there is a connection?

Obviously, it's not enough to just *have* the ethical value statements, but it certainly is the place to start. So, step one – does your organization at least have them?

Ethical Value Statements

*"It's not hard to make decisions,
when you know what your values are."*
– Roy Disney

Yes, establishing values is the first necessary step in building the organization's ethical framework. But they must be *real* values, not *lip service* values. They must be critical values in order to achieve objectives. Organizational value statements, by definition, are supposed to capture the core principles and philosophical ideas that not only inform decisions and behavior *internal* to the company, but also indicate to those *external* to the company how they intend to do business.

But you especially must pick your ethics-related value statements carefully. What do you want *ingrained* in employee's actions and behavior? What do you want your stakeholders to think of *first* when they begin to interact with the organization?

Remember, all of an organization's stakeholders want to be able to trust the organizations that they associate with. And when they go to the organization's web site, pick up a company brochure, see the profile on LinkedIn, the Better Business Bureau, or the multitude of other web-based sites, they want to get a feel of what the organization stands for.

Solid ethical value statements come in all sizes, shapes, and forms. To display this, I have included Exhibit IV in the Appendix, **Ethical Value Statements**, to provide some examples from generally well-known organizations.

But, sadly, we have to take a quick pause in this section to talk about the negative again. Perhaps even worse than having no ethics values statements, is to have them and not apply them. In other words, *empty values are worse than no values.*

I would argue that an organization with no meaningful ethical values will fail for one reason or another sooner or later. I would further argue that an organization with ethical values but no structure to ensure the values are applied, will ultimately fail as well.

The (Un)Ethical Organization chapter is full of examples. Enron's neat and tidy values were: *Communications, Respect, Integrity, and Excellence.* Yet, they displayed none of these qualities. And one of BP's value statements when the oil rig explosion occurred was: *"Safety is good business. Everything we do relies upon the safety of our workforce and the communities around us. We care about the safe management of the environment."* It also serves my point to mention BP's value statement around Courage included, *"We always strive to do the right thing."*

The bottom line: value statements are only as good as the willingness to lead and live by the values. Constant communication and reinforcement of values is required. And follow through requires the establishment and enforcement of specific accountabilities and standards of conduct *(I'm already jumping ahead here).*

A Chicago Tribune writer made a statement in an article about values and ethics that *"In every company there is some gap between professed core values and the lived values that actually guide decisions and actions. The best companies are mindful of those values gaps and take steps to narrow them."*

So, on to the next step in becoming The Everyday Ethical Organization by ensuring there are no gaps...

ORGANIZATION STANDARDS

An organization's standards of conduct *(i.e., rules)* are the extension of the organization's mission statement, values, and priorities. Adherence to the standards, just as much as values, must be ingrained in the culture of the organization.

> *"When the rules are somewhat open to interpretation, when there are grey areas – [there] can be traps for dishonesty."*
> – Dan Ariely

Simply reacting to unethical conduct when it occurs is not acceptable; the need is for proactive, preventive efforts to ensure the unethical conduct does not occur in the first place *(remember, it's about deterrence)*.

Standards of conduct are essential for all organizations, large and small. The concept works around the world in all organizations, institutions, and companies. Specific laws, regulations, and customs may vary, but the need for organization standards does not. And the standards must apply uniformly to all individuals and all levels of the organization. The credibility of the standards depends on that uniform application.

> *Well thought out standards of conduct documentation is sound business practice, a business and organization necessity.*

Detailed standards of conduct make clear to employees, and any and all other stakeholders, how the organization intends to conduct its business. Yes, the standards are specifically applicable to employees, but they also deliver an informal message to those external to the organization that the same standards apply to them when interacting with the organization. The parameters define how external stakeholders will be treated and communicate that like treatment is expected in return. It reinforces consistent behavioral expectations and boundaries in relationships.

The standards should define in detail and explain specific parameters for all conduct. The standards provide a roadmap for acceptable behavior and prohibited behavior. The standards must be in writing and communicated widely and regularly. They become the basis for orientation of new employees and are reinforced in periodic training of existing employees.

The standards must be well thought out and driven by legitimate organization and operational needs necessary to achieve its goals. The standards may be, and should be, revised from time to time, but once established they are not negotiable.

What should *not* be included in the standards? Things that are not relevant to the organization or that are not intended to be enforced. Make sure this isn't a generic "Google" standards template from the Internet that no one bothered tailoring to your organization. And for goodness sake, make sure the lawyers didn't write it and it is not way too complicated for a normal human to understand. It needs to be clear, concise, and understood by all.

ORGANIZATION STANDARDS: ETHICS

Every organization's standards may be unique, but the core ethical standards around honesty and integrity should always be present in some form. And you are about to see just how many forms it would and should appear.

Ethical standards can first be identified through a questioning process that includes the following:

√ *What are the core ethical values of the organization?*

√ *What deficiencies have occurred in the past that went against the core ethical values?*

√   *What are the behaviors that would prevent such ethical deficiencies of the past?*

√   *What are grey areas where there has been inconsistent behavior in the past?*

√   *Is there a decision tree or other resources that could be utilized for reviewing questionable behavior?*

√   *What ethical problems are anticipated by the organization in the future?*

Categories of ethical related standards for most organizations include:

o   *Personal conduct – honesty, truthfulness*

o   *Respectful relationships – harassment, bullying*

o   *Reporting integrity – financial and any other*

o   *Care of property – theft or misappropriation*

o   *Respect of privacy and security of information*

o   *Legal and regulatory compliance*

o   *Avoidance of conflicts of interest*

o   *Responsibility for health and safety*

o   *Impactful activities external to the organization*

o   *Fraud – falsification and misrepresentation*

o   *Reporting of fraud or unethical conduct*

You can tell by the extensiveness of the list *(and try to think of the full implications of each line item)* that ensuring ethical standards of conduct within an organization, particularly a large organization, takes a lot of thoughtfulness and continuous hard work.

Organizations should be prepared to update and adjust based on organization and business needs, the need for a change due to culture, internal and external events, and legal, societal, and environmental issues.

The world around us is constantly changing, therefore, each of our standards and responsibilities need to change as well. We have to make sure standards are updated continuously and communicated because as Alexander the Great said,

"Upon the conduct of each depends the fate of all."

On to the next step in becoming The Everyday Ethical Organization, how we can change our fate through enforcement...

ENFORCING ETHICAL CONDUCT

If a CEO gets away with stretching the truth with Wall Street analysts, why should anyone care about adhering to the organization's standards of conduct?

If a manufacturing company gets away with shipping products that are out of specification, why should anyone care about adhering to standards of conduct?

If the chief accountant plays fast and loose with accruals, why should anyone care about adhering to standards of conduct?

If employees falsify their time and attendance records and get away with it, why should anyone care about adhering to standards of conduct?

I'll stop; you probably get my point.

The only way to maintain high standards of ethical conduct is to enforce said standards. Zero tolerance should be the policy for ethical breaches. And standards enforcement should be administered fairly, uniformly, and consistently.

Much like values, if standards of conduct are not enforced, you might as well not have the standards. If certain individuals do not want to conform to the ethical standards of an organization, they don't belong in the organization. Period. Organizations have a choice to make and so do individuals.

Why is the military one of the most respected and trusted institutions? Aside from the reasons previously mentioned, I believe respect comes from enforcement of rules and the corrective action that results. The military is good at rule establishment and also really good at rule enforcement.

Many organizations are good at establishing standards of conduct but drop the ball when it comes to administration, i.e., enforcement of the standards. Wells Fargo, for example, has always had wonderful ethics and business conduct standards. But unfortunately, given the high number of employees and managers involved in the retail banking customer account scandal, they didn't seem to have been enforced for quite some time.

> *"People who commit fraud never think about the consequences, or they believe there will be no consequences."*
> – Biegelman and Bartow

If the above quote is true, we better start ensuring we explicitly – clearly and specifically – communicate the consequences of breaches. Let's make sure the individuals at your organization know there will be consequences and are forced to think about them!

But let's be realistic, all breaches or violations of standards are not created equal. The decision-making process around enforcement can be difficult, which is why some organizations become lax in this area. A good way of organizing the administration is to categorize offenses into several groups:

- o *Major Offenses:* An offense that the organization pre-determines that it cannot run the risk of reoccurrence. Therefore, the offense will be subject to immediate termination of employment.

- o *Sub-Major Offences:* An offense so serious that the employee will be given one chance to correct behavior and any future violation will result in termination of employment.

- o *Minor Offenses:* All other offenses still require a formal warning with the goal of correcting the behavior. If improvement does not occur, the employee will be terminated after several steps of corrective counseling.

Many corrective action procedures are written *(if at all)* in a very general way. For example, it is common to simply say the *"violations will result in disciple or corrective action up to and including discharge."* Well, I am telling you that's not good enough. The manager dealing with the infraction does not know what to do and the perpetrator has no way of knowing the seriousness of the offense nor what the consequences will be.

So, to have effective standards of conduct that are taken seriously, the standards need to be communicated with a specific indication of the consequences of a breach. In fact, I suggest you even include examples of past ethical breaches.

This approach is fairer to employees and is more likely to lead to more consistent and uniform enforcement by management. Which, by the way, are two of the top objectives of standards administration:

✓ *Uniform application:* Treat everyone the same.

✓ *Consistent application:* Applied consistently over time.

✓ *Without prejudice and bias:* To any person or group.

✓ *No arbitrary actions:* Actions without justification.

✓ *Not capricious:* No impulsive or emotional actions.

Finally, standards of conduct should be administered ethically as well. This means there is a standard of reasonableness *(often referred to as standards of just cause)* built into the process.

Fair and equitable administration and remedial action requires a process that is fact based, orderly, timely, and asks *(and answers satisfactorily)* the following questions:

Was there clear employee knowledge of the organization's standards of conduct and consequences of violations?

Was there a thorough investigation of facts and, based on the facts, was there a clear violation of the standards?

Were there any mitigating circumstances?

Was the corrective action outlined in the standards applied appropriately?

Following clear guidelines, applied uniformly to all, consistently over time, will result in behavior that supports and reinforces organization ethical values and standards.

****

I know, you thought this chapter was complete. But there is one more category of conduct that is critical to becoming The Everyday Ethical Organization we just have to discuss.

FAVORS, GIFTS, BRIBES, AND KICKBACKS

More than any other reason, I believe conflicts of interest *(one of those areas listed in the standards above)* contribute to the most unethical conduct in organizations. Why do I think conflicts of interest are a serious source of unethical issues and conduct? For one reason, my fellow accountants and auditors have reported so.

As I mentioned earlier, I conduct a Workplace Ethics Survey with all participants of my audit and ethics training seminars. See Appendix V for the QR code/link to access the **Workplace Ethics Survey**. At this point, several thousand have been surveyed across the U.S. representing a cross section of industries. Of the fifteen items in the survey covering varying opportunities for unethical conduct, the one that is consistently rated the worst offender is the item referring to *conflicts of interest.*

While there are many areas of potential conflicts, some of which will be discussed in more detail in the next chapter on organization processes and the final chapter on Total Ethical Auditing, one obvious category of conflicts that does serious damage to the ethics of an organization is the use *(either on the granting or receiving end)* of favors, gifts, bribes, or kickbacks. We'll call them FGBKs for short.

FGBKs can be subtle *(and often are)* or they can be extravagant.

> *"Though the bribe be small, yet the fault is great."*
> – Edward Coke

Sometimes they are carefully hidden or disguised; sometimes they are right there in your face. But in all forms, they can be a serious roadblock to becoming an Everyday Ethical Organization. For some organizations, FGBKs become rationalizations: we had to *"win the client at any and all cost"* or *"ends justified the means."*

Well, I want to remind you that:

> *"Financial ends never justify unethical means."*
> – Jon M. Huntsman

Hopefully you remember our discussions about Jon M. Huntsman from the *Ethical Anchors* chapter. In his book *Winners Never Cheat*, Huntsman describes a joint venture with a Far East partner. Tens of millions was invested in a new facility. After the operation began, Huntsman was informed that the local government expected annual kickbacks *(called obligations)* in order to continue the operations. The day after receiving the request, Huntsman announced that he was selling his share of the business which he ultimately did at a $3 million loss.

> *"Once you compromise your values by agreeing to bribes or payoffs, it is difficult ever to reestablish your reputation or credibility."*
> – Jon M. Huntsman

Dan Ariely in his book, *The (Honest) Truth About Dishonesty*, points out that accepting or giving gifts can be a dangerous conflict of interest, because it is a slippery slope. And, he has the studies to prove it. It is a delusion that gifts have no impact;

they influence behavior whether intended or not. And here is the important part:

The bias shifts the process from making decisions in the best interests of stakeholders... to self-interest. A conflict of interest is inherently created.

Further, Ariely's studies show that *"the magnitude of this bias increases as the magnitude of the initial favor... increases."*

Astute sales people and marketers understand the psychology of gift giving very well. The goal *is* to influence behavior, produce a feeling of indebtedness, tip the scale, and create a conflict of interest benefiting the gift giver. There is no altruism; it is all done with clever self-serving forethought. Those who deny it are flat out lying *(in addition to engaging in unethical conduct)*. And, if you are the recipient of a gift and think you are not influenced, you are lying to yourself.

The best examples *(or worst, depending on which side of the conflict of interest that you are on)* are lobbyists, representatives (reps) of the world's pharmaceutical industries (Big Pharma), and commissioned *(that's a double whammy)* financial services salespeople.

A pharmaceutical rep's job is to call on doctors in order to convince the doctor to prescribe the represented drugs to their patients. A rep may also represent medical-related equipment and devices and, again, the rep's job is to convince doctors to buy the equipment or use/prescribe the devices.

But the actual drug or device offering is often packaged with free stuff – free pads and pens, free coffee and donuts, and free drug samples. The reps know that in many cases, the free samples are anything but *"free"* – they are given to get doctors to prescribe and patients to use the drugs *(when there may very well be a generic alternative that could save the patient thousands of dollars or even a more appropriate drug therapy – a whole other can of worms).*

Then there are the free lunches for the office staff, and nice dinners at expensive restaurants, or the fancy golf outings. There are the even more serious *"education"* conferences where physicians are hired to give lectures to other physicians or consult with the drug or device maker, of course at a vacation resort with all the amenities and expenses paid. Ariely describes the process as an *"arms race"* implemented with *"military precision."* And it is all done to solidify the conflict of interest.

> *"You should always ask yourself what would happen if everyone did what you were doing."*
> – Jean-Paul Sartre

To compound the situation, even though doctors are paid to make the pitch or consult, they ignore the obvious conflict and tend to be influenced in their behavior or message. As Ariely observed, some doctors realize that they are being manipulated and others do not... *"but there is no doubt that they were."*

A pharmaceutical company owned by J&J (Janssen) is now engaged in massive lawsuits for its part in the marketing of synthetic opioids. When the marketing and selling tactics lose sight of patient and community interests and create conflicts of interests, the behavior is not only unethical, it can become a legal liability.

> *Unethical selling is creating a conflict of interest without regard to the cost/value equation of the customer and community.*

The financial services industry has a history of conflicts of interest with a host of favors and gifts in the process. A deadly combination of commissioned salespeople and a customer "perk" budget can distort whether the products being represented are in the best interest of the customer/investor or the salesperson and/or organization that they represent.

It is well recognized by most experts at this point that comparable investment products only vary in performance over the long-term by the amount of cost of the transaction *(commissions and fees)*. Since there is no difference in value, the salesperson's only weapons are the perks *(the FGBKs)*. The entire process is distorted with the thumb on the scale in favor of the product or service provider, not the investor. The salespeople know this, but the unsuspecting customer/investor may not. As John C. Bogle has said *(with a touch of sarcasm)* in explaining the conduct of those pedaling financial services products:

> *"It's amazing how difficult it is for a man to understand something if he's paid a small fortune not to understand it."*

In 2020, Goldman Sachs admitted that it had paid more than $1 billion in bribes to win work raising money for the Malaysian state-owned fund (1MDB) intended for public projects. The bribes secured hundreds of millions in commissions for Goldman Sachs but deprived the public of funds that were diverted to private individuals. The slippery slope of FGBK's cost Goldman Sachs its reputation and $5 billion in penalties.

And finally, there is Bernie Madoff and his well-publicized *"philanthropy."* There is no question in my mind that the gifts and favors were all part of the scheme to defraud investors.

Well, how did that work out for Bernie and his investors? Not well.

Ethical people and organizations do not participate in creating conflicts of interests through favors, gifts, bribes, and kickbacks. Period.

Ethics policies or standards should include a prohibition of employee acceptance of gifts from individuals they work with outside the organization. And they should include a prohibition of giving gifts *(a.k.a. bribes)* of any size, shape, or form in an attempt to influence others they work with outside the organization. Examples of language includes:

⇒ Employees are prohibited from making or authorizing payments, providing gifts, etc. that could be construed in any way as bribery.

⇒ *Employees are prohibited from granting or accepting payments, gifts, etc. from business associates.*

And the final message to consumers: Beware of anyone who wants to buy you dinner when they are trying to sell you something. Remember, *nothing* is free. It may appear to be free but may cost you your integrity... a very expensive price to pay.

****

Ethical values must be thoughtfully developed and fit the vision, mission, priorities, and stakeholders of the organization. Supporting standards of conduct should be established and the standards should be fairly, but firmly enforced. Managers should be trained in the administration so corrective action is applied uniformly and consistently. Employees should be informed of the consequences of their actions. Put it all together and...

THIS IS THE ETHICAL ORGANIZATION VALUES, STANDARDS, AND ENFORCEMENT PROPOSITION.

Critical processes are next on the list to becoming The Everyday Ethical Organization...

EXPLORE YOUR ETHICAL ORGANIZATION - VALUE, STANDARDS, AND ENFORCEMENT - CHOICES

Does the organization have clear, well thought out values that support the mission of the organization?

Are standards of conduct consistent with the organization's values, priorities, and stakeholders?

Are standards based on current, legitimate business and operational needs?

Are/were the standards developed with input from all levels and functions within the organization?

Are the standards clear, concise, and understood by all?

Are standards of conduct included in new employee orientations and reviewed annually with existing employees?

Do leaders understand the importance of fair, equitable, uniform, and consistent enforcement of the standards?

Is management trained to enforce the standards in a fair and equitable manner?

Are breaches investigated thoroughly and objectively?

Are consequences of standards violations detailed and communicated to employees, so there are no surprises?

Are employees aware of the organization's policies regarding favors, gifts, bribes, and kickbacks?

CHAPTER NINE:

ETHICAL ORGANIZATIONS

(IT'S ALL ABOUT PROCESSES)

ORGANIZATIONS CROSS THE BRIDGE into truly ethical territory when they pay extra attention to *how* they do things... their processes. Dr. W. Edwards Deming knew the importance of processes; he changed the entire business world by pointing out the importance of integrity of processes. If the process is under control, then the end product *(or service)* will take care of itself. The goal is integrity of the work – from the quality of parts, to the reliability of services, to honest, transparent decision-making.

In the previous chapter, the conduct standards setting and enforcement processes were highlighted. Well, Deming might even say it is not as much about the standards themselves as it is about the *process* of implementing and enforcing the standards – enabling the standards to become a part of and sustain an ethical culture. And as we already discussed in *The Everyday Ethical Leader* chapter, Deming also knew the importance of ethical leadership in order for a company to be successful.

Often, when leaders of organizations think about how they can reduce fraud, theft, lying, cheating, stealing, and unethical conduct in general, they instinctively jump to stricter oversight – let's add more internal auditors and perform more audits. Let's *throw auditors* at the problem and maybe it will go away. *(I am really thinking about investing in little auditors to throw into my training audiences...)*

It has been reported that Wells Fargo added hundreds more auditors in the aftermath of the retail banking scandal. Inevitably and predictably, everyone gets interested in auditing *after* the crisis. But there is little evidence that more audits leads to a higher level of ethical conduct. In fact, I'm betting that the organizations that are the most trusted have the fewest auditors. Perhaps someone needs to do a study.

> *"We want to know that someone is trustworthy or faithful. We want to be able not to have to audit their numbers."*
> – Dr. Henry Cloud

Far be it for me to devalue the importance of auditing in creating and sustaining an ethical organization *(the subject of the final chapter),* but even I think that processes are far more important. It's the processes that can really make a difference.

What we should be doing is placing the focus on improving processes that result in heightened moral and ethical awareness and better decision-making. So, besides the process of setting and enforcing organizational standards of conduct, what *are* the critical processes? There are a lot. And there isn't a better place to start in becoming an Everyday Ethical Organization than the...

****

HIRING AND ORIENTATION

"Somebody once said that in looking for people to hire, you look for three qualities: integrity, intelligence, and energy. And if you don't have the first, the other two will kill you."
– Warren Buffet

The objective of ethical organizations is to hire, retain, develop, and promote ethical employees. This emphasizes the need for processes that increase the likelihood of hiring those with high integrity and other qualities that match the values and objectives of the organization.

Performing background checks, verifying education and employment history, and contacting references can help. But conducting screening interviews with relevant ethics-related questions can help more. Ask probing questions that can provide an indication of personal and professional values of a candidate. And ensure those values match those of the organization.

However, it must be noted that the ACFE 2018 Global Study on Occupational Fraud and Abuse reported that most (96%) fraud is conducted by first time offenders. So, don't turn your new employees into *"first time offenders!"*

> *"A bad system will beat a good person every time."*
> – W. Edwards Deming

After the hiring process, new employees should be treated with a comprehensive orientation process regarding the organization's ethical values and specific standards of conduct.

Explain the basic responsibility and accountability to not only act ethically but also to report observations of ethical conduct of others. And remember, all employees become *"new"* employees when one organization acquires or merges with another. Don't skip a re-orientation process in this situation.

Hiring ethical employees and properly orienting those new recruits regarding behavioral expectations is the first step to becoming and sustaining The Everyday Ethical Organization.

****

TRAINING, TRAINING, TRAINING

> *"Character is the main object for education."*
> – Mary Wooley

Is periodic training for existing employees provided to ensure ongoing appropriate ethical behavior? Or is it a one-time thing, or conducted so infrequently that no one remembers or cares *(because if it isn't conducted very often or not at all, it must not be that important)?* Or perhaps worse, is it now an automated, computer-based training that is clicked through just to *"check the box"* that ethics training requirements have been fulfilled?

If you actually have *"live"* ethics trainings, do senior leaders attend along with everyone else and visibly show support? Better yet, do leaders participate in the instruction? Or do senior leaders rarely attend thinking *"that training is for others."*

Is the training conducted by external consultants who know very little about the organization realities, issues, and culture? Worse, is the training conducted by attorneys who focus entirely on employment law and other legal issues at the exclusion of real-life practical ethical issues and concerns?

Remember the pitfall of believing just because it is legal, it must be ethical.

There is nothing wrong with combining ethics training with legal and regulatory compliance information, but be sure to include plenty of practical content about...

➢ *Organization values*

➢ *Organization standards of conduct*

➢ *Examples of expected behavior*

➢ *Consequences of infractions*

➢ *Corrective action and discipline procedures*

➢ *Zero tolerance policies*

➢ *Duty to report non-compliance*

➢ *Reporting processes (hotlines, etc.)*

➢ *Examples of ethical challenges and how to properly handle. Include "What would you do?" case studies.*

The training process must provide an opportunity for interaction and discussion of past and current issues, as well as concerns that are anticipated in the future. Remember, this is about proactive, prevention and deterrence of unethical behavior. Haven't you heard that the number one way to prevent fraud in an organization is to talk about it? It's time to start talking... and training.

Ethics training is an opportunity to expose issues in the light of day, provide guidance, and get everyone on the same path to becoming The Everyday Ethical Organization.

****

PERFORMANCE MANAGEMENT

Adherence to the organization's values and standards of conduct should be a regular part of performance management processes – where expectations for ethical conduct are clearly established and feedback is given to employees real-time relative to their conduct.

As an internal auditor, I often refer to my preference for *coaching*, not *catching* at an organization. Auditors are mostly in the *"catching"* business – swooping in after the fact to find out what went wrong, sometimes in a crisis situation. However, it is much more productive to deal with any organizational issue as a coach, while it is happening.

Similarly, it is much more productive to deal with behavioral or conduct issues in a normal performance management or appraisal process. If there isn't one, there should be, and preferably not just in a once per year, *"check the box"* and it's over, kind of way. A solid performance management system is a critical part of an ethical organization's processes.

Most performance management systems include several steps:

✓ *Setting objectives.*

✓ *Outlining the behaviors expected to achieve the objectives.*

✓ *Identification of development needs to fill skill gaps.*

✓ *Training and development to fill the gaps.*

✓ *Periodic evaluation of results – both of goal achievement and behaviors.*

The cycle is repeated indefinitely and often. And as conduct issues are observed in the normal course of business, the issues are addressed. This is the ongoing *coaching* part. Ethical leaders are good ethics *coaches* by nature.

> *"Determine what behaviors and beliefs you value as a company, and have everyone live true to them."*
> – Brittany Forsyth

And a word of caution. Don't fall for the *"too good to fail"* performer. This is the individual that is smart, creative, innovative, and results-oriented *(really gets things done),* but is a disaster ethically – abusive, disingenuous, corrupt, self-serving, etc. Always remember, ethics trumps everything else in an ethical organization.

> *"Education without values, as useful as it is, seems rather to make man a more clever devil."*
> – C.S. Lewis

The performance management processes, including coaching and mentoring along the way, is just one more step on the journey to becoming The Everyday Ethical Organization.

****

RECOGNITION AND REWARDS

In my *Choices* book, I made a case for inspiring individuals to make decisions about their self-development in order to earn a *"Chairman's Award."* I discuss the factors needed to move closer to receiving the award of self-awareness, passion, grit, problem solving, and earning respect.

This got me thinking... why don't organizations establish a *"Chairman's Ethics Award"* that raises awareness of those who represent the qualities of The Everyday Ethicist? Recognize honesty, integrity, and character, particularly when tested under adverse circumstances. Publicly praise those who act ethically... those that live by this Thomas Jefferson quote:

> *"On matters of style, swim with the current,*
> *on matters of principle, stand like a rock."*

Looking for another reason to recommend such a program? Check out the Federal Sentencing Guidelines for corporations and other business entities convicted of federal criminal offenses:

> *"...the organization's compliance and ethics program shall be promoted... consistently throughout the organization through appropriate incentives...."*

An effective tool for developing and sustaining an ethical culture is through recognition processes for those outstanding citizens at your organization.

Recognize and reward honorable acts, particularly those performed under difficult circumstances, and you will take another step on the path of becoming The Everyday Ethical Organization.

****

PROFESSIONAL CODES

Most organizations employ various professional employees, most of whom are certified in their chosen field: auditing, accounting, information technology (IT), engineering, science, education, medicine, law, etc. And with those certifications, in any field, comes a professional code of conduct.

The question often raised is, *"Do professional codes of conduct trump organization or business standards?"* A very serious question with practical implications. And even more important when talking about ethics.

In the John C. Bogle book *(Enough)* referred to in the *Ethical Anchors* chapter, there is a chapter called, *"Too Much Business Conduct, Not Enough Professional Conduct."* Bogle makes the point that we get into trouble by rationalizing a way to avoid compliance with legitimate, well thought out professional standards that seemingly get in the way of achieving business, operational, or other organization objectives.

Accountants know darn well when they are violating professional accounting standards to make sure the numbers meet Wall Street analysts' expectations. And Engineers know darn well that they are violating professional engineering standards by falsifying emission test documents.

IT professionals have a code of conduct in regard to the respect and protection of data privacy and confidentiality. Safety professionals have a code of conduct to hold paramount the health and safety of people, property, and the environment.

And believe it or not, advertising, public relations, and marketing professionals also have a code of conduct with an objective of speaking the truth in serving the public and building and maintaining consumer trust.

The point is, these professional standards – no matter the field – exist for a reason, and the organization needs to make sure they have processes in place to acknowledge them. And that those processes support that...

Whenever there is a conflict, professional standards trump organization standards. That is the only path if you want to become The Everyday Ethical Organization.

****

ORGANIZATION STRUCTURE

Organization structure can play an important role in facilitating an ethical culture and processes. The structure is particularly important in large organizations, those that seem to have the greatest ethical risks.

There are as many kinds of structures as there are organizations *(each unique in some way),* but I believe they can be generally categorized as centralized, decentralized, or matrix driven. Each has advantages and disadvantages for business and operations purposes. But, the organization structure itself can have an influence on ethical behavior by either promoting ethical decision-making or detracting from it.

It's all about healthy checks and balances.

Centralized organizations are characterized by a concentration of power and decision-making at the top. There is a huge reliance on the character of one or a few individuals. And elevating ethics issues *(speaking truth to power)* can be difficult. It's sometimes a long, challenging road to get messages to the top of a centralized organization.

If the centralized organization is led by a Bogle, Huntsman, or Cathy, the organization ethically is in great shape. But the risks are obvious on the other side. We have already laid out plenty of examples of ethical failures of authoritarian, centralized leadership.

Decentralized organizations emphasize delegation of authority and promote individual responsibility. It's all about empowerment. Empowerment is great, but it can also lead to ethical chaos without strong values, effective standards of conduct, and supporting processes like the ones described in this chapter. But can we always count on those strong values, conduct standards, and processes to be enough? *Not necessarily.* So, here is where a matrix organization structure can help.

Matrix organizations have built-in ethical guardrails. In matrix organizations, there is a senior leadership level setting overall mission, strategy, and, hopefully, an ethical *"tone at the top."*

Then there are line functions *(product development, sales, marketing, and operations),* which tend to be decentralized around products, markets, or geographic locations, with layered groups, divisions, plants, or regional operations.

Then there are the support functions *(finance and accounting, procurement, HR, safety, information technology, audit and compliance, etc.)* both at the senior policy making level and also embedded in the decentralized units.

In a matrix organization, decentralized line functions report through the senior leadership *(CEO and senior line staff)* but the supporting functions report directly to the senior support function leaders. The dual reporting structure provides an *"ethics check"* on decisions.

We already know of the potential conflicts between driving hard to achieve business, organization, or operations objectives while maintaining professional standards and ethical means in achieving the objectives. A matrix organization can provide the check and balance.

The balanced mission is to support the line functions in achieving the overall organization goals, but to do it within ethical and professional boundaries – another step on the path to becoming The Everyday Ethical Organization.

****

HOTLINES AND WHISTLEBLOWERS

In 2018, the ACFE Global Study reported that fraud is most often detected through tips *(40%)*. Tips can come from anywhere, but over half come from employees. The ACFE Study also indicated that employing some type of confidential reporting system *(e.g., a hotline)* reduces fraud losses.

The U.S. Sarbanes-Oxley Act requires each publicly traded company to create a system for reporting misconduct. A process must be established to receive, retain, and respond to issues. The process must provide for confidential and anonymous submission and employees must be made aware of the reporting mechanisms. Although the legislation was originally designed for reporting questionable accounting and auditing matters, there are plenty of reasons for the process to apply to any and all forms of unethical conduct.

The hotline concept is not new and has been practiced by organizations, large and small, for decades. Hotlines are generally accepted as a sensible, good business and ethical organization practice. *I mean, why wouldn't every organization want to be informed of ethical breaches and provide a timely and easy process for doing so?*

The motivation should not be the legal requirements. It should be motivation enough to want ethical behavior and prompt investigation and corrective action when unethical behavior occurs. If your organization doesn't want to know about unethical behavior or breaches *(I'm picturing an executive with their hands over their ears),* you have a bigger problem to contend with.

I want to briefly mention other methods of obtaining feedback that work as well. Surveys are relatively easy to use and are an efficient means of gathering general, as well as specific information about ethics issues. You can use surveys of full employee populations to obtain an overall picture of an organization's ethical culture or use surveys to probe for specific behaviors or practices.

The Everyday Ethical Organization knows the importance of whistleblower reporting mechanisms, open door policies, and wide-ranging communication efforts to encourage honest feedback from employees. The bottom line: The Everyday Ethical Organization "loves their whistleblowers."

****

SAFETY MANAGEMENT MODEL

Effective safety management has incorporated the concept of reporting on an unsafe environment for decades. It goes something like this: Employees *(but could be any stakeholder)* are trained, encouraged, and often motivated by some type of recognition or award program, to report observed *unsafe acts* or *unsafe conditions.* The distinction between the two is that *acts* are behaviorally based, and *conditions* are based on actual physical conditions *(plant, equipment, etc.).* Often the observations are filled out on a simple card and submitted to an appropriate location/officer at the organization.

A safety model like this is considered a win-win because everyone benefits from pointing out and correcting unsafe situations. There is rarely retaliation because who is going to object to looking out for your own or someone else's health and welfare? The models are reinforced by management and supported by employees. It's proven effective; ask any competent health and safety director.

So, if you truly want to continue down the path to becoming The Everyday Ethical Organization, why not apply the safety management model to ethical acts and conditions as well? We will call this the...

****

ETHICAL MANAGEMENT MODEL

Start a program for employees to easily report *unethical acts* and *unethical conditions* that are ripe for unethical outcomes. Just as in the safety model, get everyone involved in helping your company be the most ethical company in the industry.

> *"Norms are enforced as people hold one another*
> *accountable for violating them."*
> – David Brooks

Train employees to watch daily for unethical *acts*. Define it, explain it, and provide examples: bribes, gifts, favors, kickbacks, falsification, misrepresentation, theft, abuse, harassment, breaches of data and confidential information, insider trading, accounting record manipulation, altering documents, illegal acts, etc., etc.

The same applies to unethical *conditions*. Train employees how to identify potential situations where unethical conduct may follow and provide examples: conflicts of interest situations, facility security issues, unsecured inventory and physical assets, inadequate approval processes, incomplete and missing records, lack of billing, cash, and expense controls, systems and data security vulnerabilities, unrealistic goals and pressure, customer complaints, poorly designed and administered incentive plans, lack of clear policies or policies not followed or enforced, etc., etc.

Similar to the processes we already discussed in the *"recognition and reward"* section, ensure employees not only can easily note when they observe unethical acts or conditions, but also can receive some type of recognition for reporting it. Make it a *win-win*.

Oh, and here's a place to start: the finance and accounting departments. The 2018 ACFE Global Fraud Study indicates that while financial statement fraud occurred in only 10% of cases, it caused the greatest dollar amount of damage *($800,000 median loss)*. Make sure finance and accounting employees are aware of and reporting potential unethical behavior and conditions ripe for breaches. Then, go on to other functions: engineering *(think VW)*, sales and marketing *(think Big Pharma)*, operations *(think BP)*, information technology *(think everywhere)*, purchasing and procurement *(think... well, everywhere again)*.

The Everyday Ethical Organization makes sure formal hotlines aren't the only method of communicating unethical or potential unethical acts or conditions. They are constantly thinking of new ways to empower employees with ethics.

> *"When we work as a team, other team members can act as informal monitors... and we may be less inclined to act dishonorably."*
> – Dan Ariely

****

Okay, I saved the most important, sometimes troublesome and conflicting *(and inherently unethical)* process for last...

INCENTIVES AND MOTIVATIONS

> *"When we have a mandate to be objective and an incentive not to be, our biases often win the day."*
> – Dan Ariely

Incentive plan theory is perfectly sensible. Set organization improvement goals, ratchet up personal objectives to support the goals, and offer personal monetary incentives. And POOF!! Performance improves!

Not so fast.

What often happens when organizations set improvement goals with personal incentives tied to performance?

People cheat. At least *some* people cheat.

The goal posts get moved, numbers are falsified, product quality and/or customer service declines. The list of unintended consequences is long, and it includes flat out fraud.

The well-known Fraud Triangle *(developed by renowned fraud expert Dr. Donald Cressey)* has three conditions that are generally present when fraud or unethical conduct occurs – incentive, opportunity, and rationalization.

So, just with the clear, hit you in the face terminology, a financial *"incentive"* plan provides an essential ingredient for fraud! Try to think of a major ethical crisis where financial gain was not involved either directly *(personal money in their pocket)* or *indirectly (money in their organization's pocket, and then theirs eventually).* No, this doesn't mean that *all* incentive plans result in unethical conduct, but they often do. Because sadly...

> *"Given a chance, people cheat."*
> – Dan Ariely

And incentive plans don't just provide the *incentive,* they often provide the *opportunity* and the means to cheat as well. All it takes to finalize the fraud is a little *rationalization.* And we already learned as a society we are pretty good at that part. Not a pretty picture but it is very true – and history proves it.

Professor Dan Ariely, in his book, *Predictably Irrational,* raises the question whether "social norms" or "market forces" *(e.g., incentives) "produce the most desirable outcome"* in any given set of circumstances. Well, I think Wells Fargo branch employees had a choice of serving the needs of its banking customers *(social norms)* or acting in a self-serving manner by cheating *(padding their incentives)...* And they clearly chose the latter. Would the employees have better served customers *without* the incentive scheme? *I think so.*

As most know by now, Wells Fargo branch employee incentives were based on a target number of Wells Fargo accounts per customer. The motto was *"Eight is great!"* It meant that the goal was to get each customer to enroll in eight or more bank products. Branch employees would be incentivized to work with existing customers, find out their needs, provide information, and when appropriate, sell customers more products. The bank's employees would earn incentive compensation and customers would be happy with their new bank services. POOF!! Performance objectives met, right? *No...*

Instead, Wells Fargo branch employees *"created millions of accounts in the names of its clients without their permission."* A massive fraud occurred that resulted in the termination of senior executives, including the CEO. Thousands of involved employees were also terminated, billions of fines were paid, shareholder value fell, and the bank's reputation still suffers. All because of a poorly developed incentive plan *(and complete mismanagement).* The incentive plan did not serve the company or its customers' and other stakeholders' interest well at all.

(Note, Wells Fargo has since re-designed the incentive plans to be group plans with more customer focus as well as beefed up governance and controls of plan administration. Only time will tell the rest of the story.)

Monetary incentives will only get an organization so far and, in fact, as in the Wells Fargo case, may even be self-defeating.

In ethical organizations, the real awards are not monetary.

Study after study shows that the most meaningful motivators that an organization can provide to employees are:

❖ Job opportunities with a sense of purpose.

❖ Supportive relationships.

❖ Recognition for meaningful accomplishments and a job well done.

❖ Personal growth, development, and career advancement.

❖ Leadership that empowers and respects employees.

Does anyone really think that Nobel laurate candidates create and innovate in academic, cultural, and scientific fields for the monetary rewards? *No.*

****

I know a long-time, successful Operator *(meaning restaurant owner/manager)* for Chick-fil-A. At the end of each year, the company plans and holds a pretty elaborate all Operator conference full of entertaining and educational experiences. There are opportunities to hear from the best of the best inspirational and educational speakers *(think Lou Holtz, Dave Ramsey, and Jim Collins)*. Senior executives reinforce corporate values, and strategic plans for the future are communicated and discussed. There are opportunities galore to interact and share experiences with corporate staff and fellow Operators. My impression is no expense is spared *(think Disney World Resort or Disney Cruises for thousands)*.

I asked the question, *"Wouldn't you rather have the money from that elaborate conference in your pocket?"* The answer was a resounding, *"No."* Then, I started thinking...

Would money make Operators happier with their jobs and more loyal and committed to the company?

Not likely.

Would the money make Operators better leaders?

I don't think so.

Would the money create better working relationships?

Not on your life.

Would the money make Operators more relaxed and refreshed?

I doubt it.

I assume Chick-fil-A Operators are fairly compensated *(they must be because there is very little turnover and a long list of applicants for every opening)* and to some degree financially incentivized to successfully grow their respective restaurants. However, the company clearly recognizes that money only goes so far. I'm sure there is a recognition that money does little to contribute to the consistent, well-known, acclaimed family and customer friendly values of the organization. It is clear to me that Chick-fil-A is far more interested in creating an environment where Operators and employees are motivated to care about the welfare of others. The moral of the story:

Money can't buy loyalty, trust, honesty, integrity, character, and caring.

But money can easily corrupt, lead to unintended consequences, and create conflicts of interest. And, money can easily contribute to shortcuts and mistakes that result in poor quality and service as well as misrepresentation, falsification, and other misconduct that undermine the values of the organization.

****

Unintended consequences relative to incentive plans are not exclusive to executives and sales people. I also have some personal knowledge of operational *(machining and metal fabrication in this case)* monetary incentive plans.

Once again, the theory is that it is a good thing to set goals and financially reward employees to exceed the goal. It is common for *"shop floor"* incentive plans to be based on a standard hour system. Industrial engineers determine how long it should take with defined processes, tooling, and machine tools to perform a specific job. The time allotted becomes the goal, in minutes or hours. The employee performs the job, reports the actual production time of the job, and an incentive payment is paid if the employee *"beats"* the standard. POOF!! The company gets more output and is more efficient and the employee earns more money. Everyone wins, right? *Again, no...*

What can happen is quite different, as it was in this case. First, there is a lot of energy *(and cost)* expended to study, set, and argue about the standards because ultimately money is at stake. No one is really happy in the end; the company thinks the standards should be higher and the employees want them lower.

Then, there is the quality of the product produced. Since pay is calculated based on the time spent, there is an incentive to find *(and not report)* shortcuts and invariably product/part quality suffers. When quality drops and customer complaints go up, more engineers study the problem *(more cost),* more inspectors are hired to catch the bad parts *(more cost),* and bad operators are disciplined or replaced *(even more cost).*

> *"Inspection with the aim of finding the bad ones and then throwing them out is too late, ineffective, and costly."*
> – W. Edwards Deming

Then, there is an incentive to distort things a little – fudge on the number of pieces/parts produced or falsely report the amount of time it took – since both variables can be adjusted to inflate pay. Solution again, hire more inspectors or auditors *(more cost)* because some employees cannot be trusted.

So, did the incentive plan result in more job satisfaction? Do employees now have a greater loyalty and commitment to meet and exceed organization goals? Did the incentive plan improve the ability to efficiently produce high quality products that meet and exceed customer expectations? Did the incentive plan advance the skills of employees *(no time for training now since all focus is on producing as many parts as possible)?* Did the incentive plan result in better working relationships? *Not even close.*

(Note: This particular company scrapped the incentive plan that had operated ineffectively for decades and installed a lean, total quality management system with remarkable results.)

****

Ethical organizations are careful in their design, application, and administration of incentive processes and go to great lengths to ensure that *(if they exist at all)* they contribute to honoring and supporting company values, promoting ethical conduct, and serve the interest of all stakeholders – *all necessary to become The Everyday Ethical Organization.*

****

Phew. You made it to the end of my ethical processes list. Let's recap...

- √   *Ask tough questions and hire ethical people.*
- √   *Orient people early to the organization's ethical values.*
- √   *Train forever to sustain ethical conduct.*
- √   *Focus on performance management coaching, not catching.*
- √   *Recognize and reward ethical conduct.*
- √   *Emphasize professional standards trump business goals.*
- √   *Create ethical guardrails within your structure.*
- √   *Establish hotlines and love your whistleblowers.*
- √   *Encourage reporting of all unethical acts and conditions.*
- √   *Motivate in ways that do not create ethical conflicts.*

Put them all together and...

THIS IS THE ETHICAL ORGANIZATION PROCESSES PROPOSITION.

Just one more chapter to seal the road to becoming The Everyday Ethical Organization...

EXPLORE YOUR ETHICAL ORGANIZATION PROCESSES

Does the organization have deliberate and effective processes to hire ethical people?

Are new employees sufficiently oriented to organization values and behavior expectations?

Are employees regularly trained regarding organization values, standards of conduct, and ethics issues?

Is feedback and coaching regarding ethics a part of the standard performance management process?

Are there opportunities for recognition for outstanding ethical conduct and achievement?

Do professional employees understand and practice their respective professional codes of conduct?

Does the organization structure promote checks and balances for ethical conduct?

Are there formal processes in place for employees to report ethics violations?

Are employees encouraged to report unethical conduct?

Are incentive plans designed and administered to prevent conflicts and ethical breaches?

Are employees motivated to do the right thing all the time?

CHAPTER TEN:

THE EVERYDAY ETHICAL
ORGANIZATION

(A SUMMARY)

HERE'S THE GOOD NEWS – you've already reached the summit of becoming The Everyday Ethical Organization, so this chapter is short and sweet. *(Okay, not sure about the "sweet" part, but maybe I will find some way to work that in.)*

I have spent the last four chapters inundating you with information about what unethical and ethical organizations do, so I felt some time should be given for a brief summary.

First, don't forget all of the characteristics of unethical organizations; you know, *the what-not-to-do list:*

⇒ *Don't deny and deflect when faced with questions of honesty, integrity, and character.*

⇒ *Don't be disingenuous saying one thing and doing another.*

⇒ *Don't create and innovate so fast that the interests of all stakeholders are overlooked and damaged.*

⇒ *Don't find legal loopholes, create unnecessary complexities, or use shortcuts that ultimately defraud... well, everyone.*

⇒ *Don't do things because everyone does it (or because the lawyers approve it); do them because it is the right thing to do.*

⇒ *Don't think of ethics as grey. When the smoke is blown away, it is really all black and white – right and wrong.*

These things are the epitome of an (UN) ethical organization.

Second, now that we know what an ethical organization is not... what *exactly* is it?

Just to start, an ethical organization is one where:

o *You and your family members would be proud to invest in, to lead, to work for, or to be associated with in any way.*

o *Leadership is respected for honesty, integrity, and character.*

o *There is compliance with the spirit, intent, and letter of laws and regulations.*

- *Everyone looks out for the interests of all stakeholders associated with the organization.*

- *Ethical values and conduct standards are clearly communicated and practiced by everyone, every day.*

- *There is collaboration with associates who are honest and ethical.*

- *True professionals perform their functions in compliance with the codes of conduct for their professions.*

- *Everyone is proud of being a good citizen in the communities where they reside and work.*

- *The communities are more than happy to be associated with the organization.*

Everyone wants to work for an Everyday Ethical Organization because they know they will be treated with dignity and respect, they will be compensated fairly, and the leadership will be open and honest on all matters. The leaders are clear on what they stand for and are firmly committed to their values and to the high ethical standards of conduct of their employees – *there are no exceptions.*

An Everyday Ethical Organization attracts and keeps loyal customers because they know they will be treated honestly, transparently, and fairly. There will be no games, no sales gimmicks, no false advertising or misrepresentations, and there will be total transparency – *what you see is what you get.*

And, finally, banks and investors will *"beat a path to the door"* of an Everyday Ethical Organization because they know that everything will be on the table, all dealings will be with integrity, and financial commitments will always be honored – *no matter what.*

THE EVERYDAY ETHICAL ORGANIZATION CHECKLIST

Okay, we did the *what-not-to-do list,* so let's do the *official what-to-do* list for becoming and sustaining an ethical organization:

OVERALL LEADERSHIP

√ *Attract and retain leaders with high ethical and professional standards, for themselves and others.*

√ *Set realistic expectations and provide appropriate resources to accomplish the goals and objectives.*

√ *Walk the ethical talk.*

√ *Honor commitments.*

√ *Treat others with dignity and respect.*

√ *Deal with crises openly and honestly.*

√ *Trust others and gain the trust of others.*

STAKEHOLDERS AND PRIORITIES

√ *Do no harm.*

√ *Value all stakeholders of the organization and treat them with respect.*

√ *Comply with the spirit, intent, and letter of applicable laws and regulations and promote a culture of legal compliance.*

√   *Beware of conflicts of interest and choose the welfare of stakeholders when conflict arises.*

√   *Set priorities and operate as if it is the family business.*

Values, Standards, and Enforcement

√   *Promote ethical awareness by establishing, communicating, and reinforcing ethical values.*

√   *Have written standards of conduct that are clearly communicated and uniformly and consistently applied and enforced.*

√   *Institute a zero tolerance for unethical conduct.*

√   *Investigate ethical breaches and take fair, equitable, prompt corrective action.*

√   *Ban the use of favors, gifts, bribes, and kickbacks (remember, FGBKs) in all relationships with the organization.*

Processes

√   *Select new employees and other associates after verifying ethical backgrounds and ensuring ethical values are consistent with the organization; ask the right questions.*

√   *Train employees regarding ethical related responsibilities, ethical decision-making, and accountability for reporting suspicious or unethical conduct by others.*

√   *Recognize, reward, and promote ethical behavior.*

√ *Adhere to the highest professional codes of conduct applicable to all who are associated with the organization.*

√ *Structure the organization to provide internal checks and balances.*

√ *Provide and maintain anonymous and confidential reporting procedures available to stakeholders of the organization.*

√ *Institute programs that result in a culture where reporting unethical acts and unethical conditions is a win-win situation.*

√ *Ensure that incentive plans and other motivational programs do not harm other stakeholders of the organization.*

And finally, as a safeguard suggested by Sissela Bok, I believe an Everyday Ethical Organization should ask *"Yes, but"* questions. For example,

"Yes, but"... shouldn't we tell consumers the honest truth about our products?

"Yes, but"... shouldn't we tell our investors and analysts the honest truth about the state of our affairs?

"Yes, but"... shouldn't we make sure our processes and employees are safe?

"Yes, but"... shouldn't we always make sure there are no unintended negative consequences before introducing new technology or new products?

"Yes, but"... shouldn't we make sure there is a zero tolerance for unethical conduct?

I would say there are no *"ifs, ands, or buts"* to ethical conduct, but if it helps you redirect your organization down the correct ethical path... *"Yes, but"* away.

Congratulations! You've reached the end of the ethical organization journey. You've learned what to do and what not to do as well as how to ask some tough questions. Now, it's time to take your new ethical organization *beliefs* and turn them into your organization's *destiny*.

> *"Your beliefs become your thoughts.*
> *Your thoughts become your words.*
> *Your words become your actions.*
> *Your actions become your habits.*
> *Your habits become your values.*
> *Your values become your destiny."*
> – Mahatma Gandhi

There's nothing *sweeter* than an organization that knows its beliefs, thoughts, words, actions, habits, and values become its destiny. It's time for you to help them find their way. *(I told you I would work that sweet part in, didn't I?)*

THIS IS THE EVERYDAY ETHICAL ORGANIZATION PROPOSITION.

The ethical journey continues in Chapter 11 with Total Ethical Auditing... I hope you'll continue on!

CHAPTER ELEVEN:

TOTAL ETHICAL AUDITING

(TEA)

"One... with courage makes a majority."
– Andrew Jackson

THIS CHAPTER IS ABOUT AUDITORS, primarily internal auditors, although I believe the concepts apply to external auditors as well. The content of the chapter covers the mindset of auditors, the mission of audit, and the execution of auditing. Not necessarily what they are, but what they should be.

The IIA defines internal auditing as an *"independent, objective assurance and consulting activity designed to add value and improve an organization's operations."* Internal auditors are *internal* to an organization *(obvious, I know, but even some internal auditors themselves need reminded).* External auditors, while not part of the organization, are engaged by it. The primary mission of the external auditors is to provide an independent opinion on the organization's financial statements.

Both groups of auditors have codes of ethics. The internal auditor *(IIA)* Code of Ethics' cornerstones are integrity, objectivity, confidentiality, and competency. The guide for ethics of external auditors *(AICPA)* is to serve the public interest with integrity, objectivity, independence, and due care.

Sounds good... but does it always work? Let's just say, I believe it can improve.

Broadly, I believe external auditors are not viewed as always serving the public's interest with independence and objectivity. Although the marginal reputation may have been earned over many decades, most remember the story of Enron and their external auditor, the now defunct Arthur Anderson. Arthur Anderson failed miserably at competence and independence by mindlessly colluding in the accounting fraud at Enron.

Search on public accounting and auditing scandals and many of the organizations involved in unethical conduct noted in this book will pop up – WorldCom, Tyco, HealthSouth, AIG, Lehman, Madoff, and Satyam. They all had unethical management, but they also had, at best, questionable external auditors.

More recently (2019), a Big 4 audit firm, KPMG, paid significant fines for inappropriately altering already-completed audits and illegally obtaining regulatory information. Then, if that is not bad enough, KPMG auditors cheated on regulatory mandated ethics training exams. Search on more recent public accounting scandals and examples within all Big 4 firms will come up.

Internal auditors do not fare well either, mostly by omission. Remember, internal auditors have a mission of assurance and consulting. Presumably this involves identifying and investigating high risk areas of organizations and providing help in eliminating the risks. So, where were the internal auditors at BP, Wells Fargo, VW, Boeing, Facebook, and Purdue Pharma, just to name a few?

I believe that they, and all other auditors, need a dose of *Total Ethical Auditing.*

WHAT IS TOTAL ETHICAL AUDITING?

Total Ethical Auditing *(here forward called TEA)* is my innovation of combining TQM concepts with methods of internal audit to improve personal, leadership, and organization ethics. *(Not surprising that those are the previous sections of this book, right?)*

The founding father of TQM, W. Edwards Deming, and the principle objectives of TQM were identified in the *Ethical Leadership* chapter and included serving the interests of stakeholders through processes and leadership with integrity.

TEA is also just a short step from my trademarked Total Quality Auditing (TQA) approach to internal audit. TQA focuses on auditing culture and conduct, serving stakeholder needs, and performing audit work efficiently and effectively, with great leadership.

TEA narrows the focus of internal auditing to the personal, leader, and organization behaviors and processes that have ethical implications – the behaviors that get in the way of serving all stakeholders of an organization.

Throughout this chapter, we will draw on the concepts and examples of previous chapters – the ethical anchors, ethical mirages, and the do's and don'ts of ethical leadership and ethical organizations. The chapters related to ethical organizations introduced many approaches and processes that should help to support and sustain organization ethics. But this chapter will cover how internal auditors can help in that effort.

Establishing and sustaining ongoing organization ethics is particularly difficult because organizations inherently deal with many people with different backgrounds, experiences, and personal values – all blended together. Throw in disingenuous leaders, conflicts from competing interests, counterproductive financial incentives, and authoritative relationship dynamics, and things can get *even more* complicated.

Now enter internal audit – with the unique and difficult challenge of identifying, understanding, and mitigating ethical risks with the objective of improving overall ethical conduct. I believe there are a number of internal audit shops that will shy away from even touching the area of ethical risks – because of the perceived subjective nature and inherent challenges. But that's no longer an excuse. I am here to change the internal auditor mindset, mission, and practice of auditing ethics through TEA.

****

It's time to:

THINK AND PLAN LIKE A FRAUD EXAMINER

EXECUTE LIKE AN INVESTIGATIVE JOURNALIST

MITIGATE LIKE A COACH

BE A TOTAL ETHICAL AUDITOR

Let me expand on each a little bit more here:

1) *Think and plan like a fraud examiner* – focusing on areas of opportunity where people are motivated to commit unethical acts and where they are likely to find rationalizations for their actions.

2) *Execute like an investigative journalist* – deeply investigating those areas of opportunity and motivation that create high risks and negative impact to stakeholders.

3) *Mitigate like a coach* – consulting, counseling, mentoring, and training to improve ethical conduct necessary to achieve organization goals the right way *(the first time)*.

4) *Be a Total Ethical Auditor* – displaying a unique set of personal and professional ethical qualities required to perform TEA.

This unique framework and mindset for TEA will enable internal auditors to have a great impact and to truly fulfill their mission to add value and improve an organization's operations.

> *"Don't worry about the darkness – turn on the light and the darkness automatically goes."*
> – David Lynch

Step One: Think and Plan Like a Fraud Examiner

The word fraud is defined by *Merriam-Webster* as:

o *Deceit, trickery, and the intentional perversion of truth in order to induce another to part with something of value or to surrender a legal right.*

o *An act of deceiving or misrepresenting.*

o *A person who is not what he or she pretends to be.*

o *A thing that is not what it seems or is represented to be.*

Think imposter, sham, fake, con, fiddle, gyp, hustle, scam, sting, swindle, double-deal, subterfuge, trick. *I think you get it.*

Fraud has been synonymously used in the context of this book as lying, cheating, stealing, financial engineering, misrepresenting, false advertising, misleading marketing, using FGBK *(favors, gifts, bribes and kickbacks),* and exploiting loopholes and shortcuts in general.

The word fraud *(or some derivative of it)* has been used 64 times so far in this book. *(And no, I am not talking about financial derivatives, which are ripe for fraud themselves.)* The many references to fraud in this book include the 2008 financial crisis, the opioid crisis, and the college admissions scandal, as well as insider trading, accounting and audit shenanigans, safety shortcuts, and data security and privacy breaches.

Specific *"frauds"* mentioned were Enron, Worldcom, Tyco, Madoff, Purdue Pharma, Wells Fargo, Volkswagen, Goldman Sachs, Theranos, along with their many *disingenuous leaders.*

Fraud has also been described in this book using means like the fraud triangle, and descriptions of the various fraud mentalities, such as the *"everybody does it"* or the *"it's all grey area"* mentality. We've discussed the reporting of fraud, the covering up fraud, and the many consequences and costs of fraud.

What does all this mean to you?

Fraud – in its various forms, definitions, or explanations – is a BIG thing in this world and therefore should be a BIG thing to auditors. Even if you aren't a Certified Fraud Examiner *(although I highly recommend it)*, it's time to start acting like one. Let's talk about what that means.

ETHICAL RISK ASSESSMENTS AND RED FLAGS

I have found throughout my career that internal auditors tend to focus mostly on the past, the routine, and the minor issues at their organizations. To substantiate my observations, I poll internal auditors often about how they spend their time and how they believe they *should* be spending their time to add more value and contribute more.

Auditors consistently report that they are spending time in low risk areas and that they spend little time in the critical, high risk areas. While they answer *"absolutely"* to the question of if they *should be* auditing culture and ethics, they answer *"rarely"* to the question of if they *are actually* doing it. There is something blaringly wrong with this picture.

Internal auditors are not consistently paying attention to the *red flags* – the really important areas of potential unethical conduct. So, I've created a *"Red Flag Assessment"* to help with this process, combining some of our known and available risk analysis/assessment tools.

The very first step in this new assessment is to identify categories of ethical risk *(i.e., the red flags)* for your organization. We will elaborate on all the types of red flags later on in this section, but here are some examples of "Ethical Risk Categories" to get you started: *Disingenuous Leadership, Suspect Accounting Processes, and Aggressive Incentives and Compensation.*

At the center of each of the assessments that follow is the Ethical Risk Category you are analyzing.

THE FRAUD TRIANGLE ASSESSMENT

OPPORTUNITIES, INCENTIVES/PRESSURE, AND RATIONALIZATION

Reference was made earlier in this book to the Fraud Triangle concept and the three conditions that are generally present when fraud or unethical conduct occurs – *opportunity, incentive or pressure, and rationalization.*

It only makes sense that the path to the high risks starts with areas of the greatest *opportunity* for unethical conduct, where there are the greatest *incentives or pressure* to commit unethical acts, and in areas where people tend to *rationalize* their unethical behavior.

****

Call this piece the *Fraud Triangle Assessment:*

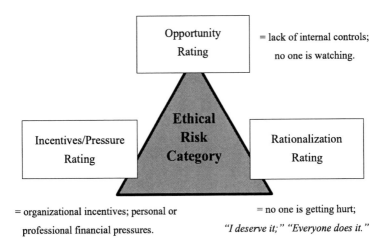

Let's go through an example to help explain this first risk assessment.

For the Ethical Risk Category of *Suspect Accounting Processes,* what is the opportunity for this risk to exist? *(i.e., lack of controls)* – what is the pressure for this to exist? *(i.e., aggressive financial targets to hit)* – and what is the possibility for rationalizations to exist? *(i.e., mentality of "everyone does it" is prevalent across the organization.)*

Any ratings can be used – but I suggest a 1 (low risk) to 5 (high risk) rating scale to keep it simple. Add up your three ratings to get your overall *Fraud Triangle Assessment* rating for each Ethical Risk Category you have identified for your organization.

(We will discuss how to analyze the ratings for the Fraud Triangle Assessment below; keep going to put it all together.)

****

THE RISK IMPACT ASSESSMENT

RISK SIGNIFICANCE, LIKELIHOOD, PERVASIVENESS, AND COUNTERMEASURES

Martin Biegelman and Joel Bartow in their book, *Fraud Prevention and Internal Control,* provide further conceptual tools to narrow the search for truly high risk areas including:

⇒ A determination of the *significance* of the risk *(how much damage can be done);*

⇒ The *likelihood* that the unethical conduct will occur;

⇒ The potential *pervasiveness* of the risk throughout an organization;

⇒ And the degree to which there are built-in *countermeasures* that might prevent the unethical conduct *(or not).*

Call this piece the *Risk Impact Assessment:*

To continue with our first example for the Ethical Risk Category of *Suspect Accounting Processes,* what would be the rating (again 1 – low to 5 – high) for the significance, the likelihood, the pervasiveness, and the countermeasures in place for this risk? *(For countermeasures if there are few countermeasures in place (i.e., no controls, this would be rated a 5.)* Add up your four ratings to get your overall *Risk Impact Assessment* rating for each Ethical Risk Category.

(We will discuss how to analyze the ratings for the Risk Impact Assessment – with the Fraud Triangle Assessment – next. Again, stick with me to put it all together!)

****

THE RED FLAG ASSESSMENT

ETHICS FAILURE AND EFFECTS ANALYSIS

The very last step is to apply a version of the old Six Sigma problem solving tool called an Ethics Failure and Effects Analysis. *(The original tool is called a Failure Modes and Effects Analysis.)*

Take your ratings for each Ethical Risk Category based on the Fraud Triangle Assessment factors *(opportunities, incentive/pressure, and rationalization) and* the Risk Impact Assessment factors *(significance, likelihood, pervasiveness, and countermeasures)* and put them all together to create a calculation or graphic visualization of the overall ethics failure risk by category.

Call this the *Red Flag Assessment:*

Ethical Risk Category	Fraud Triangle Assessment Rating	Risk Impact Assessment Rating	Overall Ethical Failure Risk Rating
Disingenuous Leadership	13	14	<u>27</u>
Suspect Accounting Processes	11	19	<u>30</u>
Aggressive Incentives	13	19	<u>32</u>

As you can see, our example of *Suspect Accounting Processes* has a fairly high "Overall Ethical Failure Risk Rating" and most likely should be included in our Internal Audit Plan one way or another. Note, the more Ethical Risk Categories you use, the more you will be able to compare and rank from high to low, to clearly see where you should be spending more of your time. This is the TEA approach to creating a *Red Flag Assessment* for the target of audits.

****

As promised, let's now discuss what Ethical Risk Categories *(i.e., Red Flags)* could exist at your organization... *and would be subject to the assessments above.*

DISINGENUOUS LEADERS

"Power without sufficient accountability leads to corruption."
– Biegelman and Bartow

Most, if not all, senior leaders have the *opportunity* for unethical conduct by the nature of the position. They are typically financially *incentivized* so there is a strong motive. And successful senior leaders are notorious for big egos, which tend to more easily *rationalize* behavior. So, disingenuous leaders are automatically pretty *high risk* on the Fraud Triangle Assessment.

What about the Risk Impact Assessment? Well, disingenuous senior leaders' decisions are clearly significant *(big dollar impact),* they may likely waiver ethically because of financial incentives *(e.g., stock options),* their decisions are certainly pervasive with impact, and with autocratic senior leaders, there are often few countermeasures *(i.e., few checks and balances).* So, clearly disingenuous leaders are also high risk on this assessment.

I mean, just think about how Bernie Madoff, Dennis Kozlowski, or Elizabeth Holmes would have rated. Or how about the board members of Bernard L. Madoff Investment Securities LLC *(yes, there was one board member),* Tyco, or Theranos? Trust me, with this assessment you will get similar high risk ratings.

Rate your senior leadership and the board with an objective scale combining all known factors. Review senior leadership and board member characteristics. Do they lead with integrity that is pervasive throughout the organization like a Bogle, Cathy, or Wegman? Or are they more like a Madoff, Kozlowski, or Holmes? Or somewhere in between?

Look back at the *(Un)Ethical Organization* chapter's Disingenuous Leadership section for all the traits and characteristics. Also review all the *"Big Me"* and *"Rationalizer"* qualities mentioned in the *Ethical Choices* chapter. Or use this list from Eugene Soltes' book, *Why They Do It,* which outlines many red flags for the misconduct of leaders:

✓ *They are so wrapped up in themselves (the Big Me's) that they cannot see the damage that they are causing to themselves and others.*

✓ *They are so egocentric and autocratic that they do not seek or accept advice and counsel from others.*

✓ *They intentionally surround themselves with weak or conflicted subordinates – the "lapdogs."*

✓ *They are under the direction of incompetent or conflicted board members.*

✓ *They manage by fear. (Remember, fear leads to wrong numbers, shortcuts, unhappy customers, and self-preservation.)*

✓ *They set arbitrary goals without necessary resources and demand achievement of the goals by any means.*

✓ *They make hasty, impulsive decisions and don't stop to thoughtfully consider the implications.*

✓ *They deal in an impersonal, global context and could care less about the impact on stakeholders they will never meet.*

✓ *They do the cold hard calculation of the potential costs and potential benefits and decide that the financial benefits far outweigh the costs of getting caught for unethical conduct.*

✓ *They never consider negative outcomes, or they just don't care if there is one. They are huge risk-takers.*

✓ *They have no sense of guilt; it's all "business" and unethical conduct is rationalized away.*

And lastly...

✓ *They may talk about ethics, but they do anything and everything but behave ethically.*

History tells us there is a high likelihood of senior management participation or knowledge in major ethical breaches. Disingenuous senior executives have been involved in scandals resulting in tens of thousands of job losses, tens of billions of investor losses, hundreds of millions in fines, and in many cases, prison time for orchestrating the frauds. And many families and entire communities have been devastated by their fraudulent conduct. Internal auditors: don't underestimate the damage that can be done by this type of leadership; start assessing it properly.

Disingenuous leaders sometimes are CFOs, Chief Accounting Officers (CAOs), or others in senior finance positions, so let's take another minute and discuss them specifically...

DISINGENUOUS FINANCE AND ACCOUNTING LEADERSHIP

"A compensation structure that heavily emphasizes the bottom line creates an environment that sometimes encourages accounting chicanery."
– Howard Schilit

Sadly, the finance and accounting functions are ripe for fraud because it is mostly *"all about the money"* and *"hitting the numbers."* It is about pressure to meet or exceed internal forecasts or Wall Street analysts and investors expectations.

The pressure is often felt by senior finance leaders simply because of job security; people get fired all the time for failure to meet financial objectives. Or, pressure can come because of personal financial rewards for many across the organization; periodic incentive payments *(bonuses, stock options, etc.)* are awarded based on meeting or exceeding financial goals.

The pressure to perform can lead to aggressive accounting practices or out and out fabrication, falsification, and misrepresentation of financial statements. The famous accounting scandals the last couple of decades are plentiful:

- Waste Management reported $1.7 billion in fake earnings by playing with depreciation schedules.

- Enron hid huge financial losses using mark-to-market and off-the-books accounting to the tune of a $1.2 billion value write-off.

- WorldCom inflated assets by almost $11 billion by capitalizing instead of expensing cost items and also inflated revenues by making false entries.

- Tyco inflated company earnings by over $500 million and covered up personal expenses inappropriately charged to the company ($150 million).

- HealthSouth inflated earnings by over $1.8 billion.

Then there was AIG manipulating stock prices and committing a massive accounting fraud of $4 billion, Lehman Brothers hiding $50 billion in loans to inflate sales revenue, and Bernie Madoff keeping two sets of books to trick investors out of $64.8 billion.

There was the Satyam scandal, an Indian IT services and accounting firm based out of Hyderabad, India with a calculated, choreographed financial fraud involving inflated revenue, forged documents, fictitious headcount, fabricated bank statements, understated liabilities, and overstated margins and earnings to the tune of $1.5 billion.

And as I am writing this book, a newly uncovered accounting scandal by Wirecard, a German payment processor and financial services provider, where $2.2 billion cash is "missing," among other potential accounting irregularities.

> *Finance and accounting can become the unethical means to achieve the desired outcome.*

So, how do finance and accounting leaders fit on the Red Flag Assessment? There can be plenty of opportunity and incentives and the impact is obviously significant. Therefore, finance and accounting leaders should be assessment candidates. Watch for CFOs, CAOs, and other finance leaders that:

- *Are under pressure to "deliver the numbers" to meet forecasts, budgets, and expectations.*

- *Have a low regard for finance and accounting professional codes of conduct.*

- *Have an "everybody does it" and/or "everything is grey" mentality.*

- *Have little knowledge and/or regard for Financial Accounting Standards Board (FASB) Generally Accepted Accounting Principles (GAAP). (Or are continuously "stretching" the application of accounting principles.)*

❖ *Hire external auditors who lack integrity and independence or that seem to have too close of a relationship with the auditors.*

❖ *Are obsessed with tax avoidance by any means.*

❖ *Propose overly complex transactions continuously.*

❖ *Are in a constant "business crisis mode" of lost market share, declining revenues, excessive costs, and bottom-line losses.*

These disingenuous finance leaders can have a ripple effect throughout the accounting function, leading to a series of additional red flags...

SUSPECT ACCOUNTING PROCESSES

"Financial fraud can be fatal to a company and to those involved."
– Biegelman and Bartow

Be aware of and alert to environmental conditions including:

⇒ *Pressure from too much debt.*

⇒ *Loss of market share.*

⇒ *Declining revenue, increasing costs, lower earnings.*

It is sometimes easier to cut corners than to be totally honest about the state of the business.

Be aware of and alert of the most common ways to *"cook the books"* or engage in *"financial engineering"* including:

• *Overstating inventories, assets, and income.*

• *Using misrepresented timing differences.*

- *Failure to recognize bad debts and failure to recognize negative impacts of "mark-to-market."*

- *Capitalizing expenses and concealing liabilities.*

- *Recording fictitious revenue or premature recognition of revenue.*

Internal auditors, it's time to get engaged in the important management judgment and policy details such as revenue recognition policies and practices. Review all accounting estimates requiring subjective judgements. Look for unreasonable restructuring charges, creative acquisition accounting, or unrealistic reserves.

Ensure you always understand the motives for changes in accounting policies and practices. Watch for unsupported accounting entries, missing documentation, or misapplication of accounting principles. Beware of complex financial transactions, organization structures, and creation of new legal entities.

Use your common sense auditor judgment. Financial results that are too good to be true and inconsistent with the underlying operating facts and conditions could be a huge issue.

And remember the Red Flag Assessment. All of these suspect accounting processes get fueled by opportunity *(lack of controls and oversight)*, limited only by imagination *(rationalization)*, with all kinds of motivations, mainly external pressure and financial incentives. And this is compounded by the significant and pervasive impact accounting processes have to an organization.

Have I already mentioned the impact financial incentives can have on leaders and processes? (That's a joke, by the way. You should be almost tired of it by now.) Let's dive into that red flag a little further...

AGGRESSIVE INCENTIVES AND COMPENSATION

When it comes down to it, incentive plans have been at the bottom of major frauds for decades. So, auditors, it is time to fully understand the important connection between incentives and compensation and financial and operating goals.

As we already reviewed, senior leaders and finance and accounting personnel are often under pressure to report favorable financial results due to the connection to bonuses and stock options.

Sales personnel who are incentivized to sell more products or services are also incentivized to play games with the target setting process, use unethical means to get results, and misrepresent the actual results.

Operations personnel who are incentivized to produce more products faster or deliver more services faster, are also incentivized to manipulate the goal setting process, take shortcuts in quality, and misrepresent the actual products produced or services completed.

The theory that setting aggressive targets and incentivizing the workforce to achieve the targets and *"living happily ever after"* was debunked decades ago by W. Edwards Deming. Deming taught everyone that incentivized work leads to shortcuts, poor quality, falsification and misrepresentation, unhealthy competition rather than productive collaboration, dissatisfied customers, and major ethical crises. But, unfortunately, not everyone listened.

Internal Auditors, your number one choice should be to recommend alternate motivators at your organization and the elimination of incentive plans. If this is not reasonable, your second choice *(and this is not really a choice but is a MUST)* is to spend a lot of time reviewing to ensure that incentive plan designs are aligned with legitimate organization objectives, are consistent with sound risk management, and guard against unintended consequences. Focus on:

o *How targets/goals are set and changed.*

o *How incentive plans are approved, communicated, and administered.*

o *How financial and/or operating results incentivized are reported and audited.*

o *How incentives are calculated and paid.*

The bottom line is this: Performance-based compensation plans are a bright red flag when the plan encourages or enables unethical conduct. Perform your Fraud Triangle, Risk Impact, and Red Flag Assessment to see how your organization's incentive and compensation plans rate.

On to a more general ethical risk category that is critical for an organization's ethical success...

DEFICIENT STANDARDS OF CONDUCT

I'll be brief in this section. The failure to effectively establish, administer, and enforce organization ethical standards of conduct are an immediate red flag. Internal auditors look closely if your organization:

- *Fails to express the importance of ethical conduct in mission or value statements.*

- *Has no standards of conduct regarding personal ethical behavior.*

- *Has standards but fails to require the report of ethical breaches.*

- *Does not fully investigate the breaches and take appropriate corrective action.*

- *Lacks clear communication of consequences of ethical breaches including a zero-tolerance policy.*

- *Lacks training regarding standards of conduct.*

- *Lacks consistent and uniform enforcement of standards of ethical conduct.*

Without ethical standards of conduct, or with standards that are deficient, the rationalization risk rating within the Fraud Triangle Assessment will be inherently high. Individuals will rationalize unethical behavior due to lack of rules and guidance being in place. And the countermeasures risk rating within the Risk Impact Assessment will also be high. Ethical standards of conduct are one of the best countermeasures an organization can deploy.

Even if solid ethical standards of conduct exist, there still may be indicators the organization's environment is an ethical risk...

ENVIRONMENTAL AND BEHAVIORAL ISSUES

"Shh. Listen to the sounds that surround you."
– Pete Seeger

Some common environmental conditions and behavioral characteristics can be ripe for unethical results. Internal auditors – look closely if your organization:

√ *Invests little in training and education. Little emphasis on training leads to mistakes, out of control processes, and poor conduct.*

√ *Is engaged in aggressive cost cutting. Cost cutting can lead to cutting corners and questionable practices.*

√ *Has remote locations, field offices, regional or overseas locations. They sometimes work by their own standards or those of others (external) that they are around.*

√ *Has individuals and groups with a high level of interaction with external organizations (e.g., sales, purchasing, traders, brokers, contract administrators, etc.). Those who are unusually close to vendors, customers, or contractors may be more loyal to external influences and may adopt the conduct standards of others external to the organization.*

√ *Contracts external auditors who are more interested in promoting the business relationships than providing independent, competent assurance.*

√ *Has no meaningful method of feedback from stakeholders (whistleblowers) or retaliates against those who report ethical breaches.*

√ *Obstructs regulators from doing their jobs rather than collaborating to raise the bar of lawful, ethical conduct by all.*

√ *Has strained relationships between management and employees often exhibited by high turnover.*

You may recognize the above list if you have studied TQM *(or TQA through me)* previously. This list includes many of W. Edwards Deming's TQM "warnings" *(my word, not his)* that would preclude the success of an organization. And this is one of the most important lists I go through with internal auditors to ensure they are properly assessing and auditing culture.

Each one of these items increases the ratings on our Assessments: Opportunity, Rationalization, Significance, Likelihood, Pervasiveness – and could add up to an extremely high ethical risk if these environmental or behavioral red flags are present at your organization.

We've talked about ethical risks and red flags related to leaders, processes, and standards, but we can't forget those that are at the "top" of all of these at an organization...

BOARDS AND (UN) ETHICS

"A board can't just be some important people we know."
– Patrick Lin

Board members seem to be as surprised as everyone else when organization (un)ethical crises occur. How can that be when the board's responsibilities include such things as selecting the senior leaders who set the ethical *"tone at the top?"* The board's responsibilities include duties such as:

⇒ *Determining the organization's mission statement and values to be promoted throughout the company.*

⇒ *Enhancing the organization's public image.*

⇒ *Ensuring fiscal accountability.*

⇒ *Establishing a governance system and ensuring that internal controls are effective.*

⇒ *Protecting the organization's assets.*

⇒ *Maintaining integrity.*

⇒ *Looking out for the interests of shareholders and relevant stakeholders.*

Board members serve on committees with responsibilities for establishing and applying ethics and compliance guidelines, evaluating organizational risks, reviewing executive compensation, and providing oversight of the audit function.

So, with all these responsibilities that directly or indirectly influence the ethical culture of an organization, why do ethical breaches with responsible boards ever occur? The realty is – don't expect the board to add much value in establishing an ethical culture or heading off unethical conduct.

The culture and conduct is normally a function of organization leaders *(formal and informal),* not the board. That does not mean the board members are not ethical; they simply are sometimes not engaged. Board members are often in it for the prestige, perks, and paycheck and lack the time, interest, independence, and competence to effectively add value when dealing with ethical issues.

Remember the case of the compensation of the CEO of the Florida Coalition Against Domestic Violence (FCADV). The

FCADV Board approved $7.5 million in compensation and benefit payments to the CEO over a three-year period. The Board members *trusted* the CEO and, when pressed, they claimed that they simply did not know what they were approving.

> *"With a large part of my income depending on [XYZ company] success, I would probably not be as critical...*
> *of the [company's] actions."*
> – Dan Ariely

Aren't board members supposed to oversee the organizations that they serve? Aren't they supposed to raise the tough questions? Well, yes, but if they are not told the truth, don't expect any ethical miracles from board members.

I believe the only hope is that internal auditors find and report the ethical truth to the board. Auditors must be fully aware that the board does not necessarily hear the unvarnished truth from senior executives, particularly in sensitive areas like ethical conduct. Assess the ethical risk of your board, and then take the appropriate actions needed to engage them.

And if the board will not accept the truth from auditors about unethical conduct, the auditor has the responsibility to become a whistleblower, filing a report with the appropriate government body. Silence is not golden within TEA, and is not an option for internal auditors, under any circumstance.

> *"Don't be afraid of the truth."*
> – John A. Vucetich

On to one last, big ethical risk category that often gets overlooked, especially in those "move fast and break things" organizations...

(UN)ETHICS AND TECHNOLOGY

The ethics of technology is a large and complex issue. So, what are the *primary* technology-related issues that are candidates for TEA? I'll break them into two main parts – the technology itself and the impacts of the technology on others.

The *"technology itself"* issues involve the actual development of new technology. For example, should we have Global Positioning System (GPS) tracking, self-driving cars, full-body airport scanners, genetically modified organisms, or a nuclear bomb? Big questions for philosophers, but not likely for internal auditors. *(But this is not to say you shouldn't get involved at all in product development.)*

But I do believe we, as internal auditors, have an important role to play in the *"impacts of technology on others"* issue. We should be ensuring the technology is consistent with organization ethical values and does not create risks and adverse consequences for individuals, organizations, and communities – i.e., the public at large.

Let's use some examples from this book. Internal auditors would not necessarily become involved in how new opioid drugs are developed – but we should be involved if the drugs are falsely advertised, marketed, or misleading in any way to regulators, doctors, distributors, or patients.

Internal auditors would not become involved in whether offshore oil drilling is developed and expanded *(we would most likely leave this to the engineers)* – but we should absolutely be involved to make sure the technically complex operations are safe for employees, communities, and the environment.

Internal auditors would not become involved in whether new cloud based on-line banking products are developed and marketed – but we should ensure that the related complex system infrastructure is secure and personal data is protected.

So, what are some of the major categories of significant technological developments today with ethical risks/red flags we should be analyzing? There are eight we will go through *(in no particular order)*:

1) Data Security and Privacy

2) Artificial Intelligence

3) Drones, Robots, and Autonomous Things

4) Connected Devices

5) Big Data and Analytics

6) Intellectual Property

7) Cybercrime

8) Cryptocurrency

Make sure to run each through the earlier risk assessments to truly identify where you need to be focusing when it comes to technology risks impacting your organization.

#1 - DATA SECURITY AND PRIVACY

Information technology (IT) innovations have clearly outpaced the ability *(or will)* to secure enormous amounts of data and protect rights to personal data. Massive hacks and security breaches occur almost daily, mostly with organizations that do not invest in the resources to design and implement secure systems. If there is any doubt, check out this site:

https://www.informationisbeautiful.net/visualizations/worlds-biggest-data-breaches-hacks/

IT audits should not only determine whether the appropriate IT controls are in place to protect corporate assets, but they should also ensure system integrity relative to collecting, storing, sharing, and disposal of customer data. Internal auditors should confirm the company has IT policies and processes that are aligned with the organization's ethical values and that protect all stakeholders of the organization.

#2 - ARTIFICIAL INTELLIGENCE

Artificial intelligence (AI) is the branch of computer sciences that emphasizes the development of intelligence machines that think and act like humans. But AI is only as good as its data and design. Ethical responsibility for the outcomes of AI lies with designers, programmers, and their leaders.

The good news: AI produces consistent, predictable results usually with greater efficiency. AI scoring systems use a wealth of data and can separate legitimate transactions from fraudulent ones, thereby detecting fraud.

The bad news: AI is only as ethical as the design assumptions. AI has no empathy when things go wrong. Data and design inaccuracy can lead to unintended consequences *(garbage in means garbage out)*. Oh, and fraudsters can use AI too, and can also *"mess"* with yours.

TEA includes transparent auditing of the AI policies and procedures to ensure compliance with organization objectives and values and to ensure applications truly benefit the organization *and* its stakeholders.

#3 - DRONES, ROBOTS, AND AUTONOMOUS THINGS

Drones *(unmanned aerial vehicles)* can be used as excellent tools for hobbies or businesses, greatly improving efficiency *(e.g., real estate listing photography)*. But they can also be used to spy illegally, becoming a concern for privacy and security.

Robots, machines capable of carrying out a complex series of actions automatically, can lead to efficiency in simple, repetitive tasks or in environments hazardous to humans. But just as with AI or drones, they are only as good as the programming behind the technology.

I mentioned in an earlier chapter that one of my favorite TED-Ed videos to show in my ethics trainings is called "The Ethical Dilemma of Self-Driving Cars." This video brings up several challenging questions related to the programming of self-driving cars: Should the car be programmed to prioritize your safety or minimize danger to others? Should the car factor in the ages and particulars of the lives of the passengers in each car?

Patrick Lin, the creator of the TED-Ed video, an associate professor of philosophy, and the director of the Ethics and Emerging Sciences Group at California Polytechnic State University, poses the following:

If a small tree branch pokes out onto a highway and there's no incoming traffic, we'd simply drift a little into the opposite lane and drive around it. But an automated car might come to a full stop, as it dutifully observes traffic laws that prohibit crossing a double-yellow line. This unexpected move would avoid bumping the object in front, but then cause a crash with the human drivers behind it.

Should autonomous vehicles be programmed to obey the law or avoid harmful crashes? Ethics and lawfulness are not always the same. As Lin states, *"...ethics and law often diverge, and good judgment could compel us to act illegally."*

Hopefully you remember those *"Yes, but"* questions I introduced in Chapter 10. This is another place they could be used to ensure thoughtfulness in the applications of drones, robots, and autonomous things at your organization. Internal Auditors need to review the ethical impact of the design and use of these technologies on all stakeholders.

#4 - CONNECTED DEVICES

GPS, a satellite-based radio navigation system owned by the United States government, is increasingly being used by organizations to monitor and track locations and movement of people and things. Inherently, the use of this information raises ethical concerns related to security and privacy.

Smart home devices which connect to the Internet and can be controlled and monitored remotely also have ethical issues attached. Think of popular devices like the Amazon Echo, Google Nest Cameras, Ecobee Thermostats, Ring Doorbells, and so many more. Each of these connected devices are constantly listening, tracking, and monitoring and, while they can make individuals and home monitoring more effective or efficient, they also come with many security, privacy, and information usage concerns.

Specialized internal auditors can perhaps review product designs to mitigate the risk of unintended consequences, such as ensuring access controls are in place to avoid the threat of hacking. But just as importantly, internal auditors need to ensure that strict policies are established that confirm legitimate business purposes for data collected, while also securing the data and protecting stakeholder privacy rights.

#5 – BIG DATA AND ANALYTICS

As the scale and ease of accumulating big databases of information increases in a world that wants to monetize everything, ethics enters the picture. Organizations need to be reminded of the ethical implications and asked the tough questions, like *"who owns all the data that is being analyzed? And what all will I be doing with the data?"*

After reading a recent *(September 2020)* update on Google acquiring the fitness tracking, Fitbit, I realized those tough questions absolutely need to be asked during an acquisition such as this.

The deal has already been receiving tough scrutiny because of *"perceived privacy concerns"* including the health data that will be obtained from Fitbit users believed to be utilized in the future by Google for targeted advertising purposes. While a Google spokeswoman said, *"This deal is about devices, not data,"* given the history of how big tech companies have used data previously, it is not surprising that this statement is not 100% trusted by consumers.

Fortunately, there are a few principles that internal auditors can use to help in establishing policy and guiding actions around big data. The first principle: People should have control *(with clear rules)* over their personal information – no *"gotcha"* allowed. Next, there needs to be ethical considerations and rules for what is shared and what is not, and the owners of the data should be aware of exactly how the data is used. And lastly, big data should not be combined with algorithms that produce unethical biases.

We, as auditors, need to have a voice in the process to ensure big data is always used ethically. I can only hope the internal auditors at Google remind their leaders that the acquisition was about *"devices, not data"* when the time comes to increase profit.

#6 – INTELLECTUAL PROPERTY

Intellectual property (IP) is protected by laws, including patents, copyrights, and trademarks. IP is often intangible because it concerns creations of the mind, such as inventions, literary and artistic works, designs, software programs or codes, and symbols, names, and images used in commerce.

Internal auditors can help inventory all the IP that is either owned or utilized by your organization. Ensure that policies and procedures regarding the use, storage, transfer, file sharing, and security of IP are in place to protect the rightful owners. And most importantly, ensure that others' IP is not illegally obtained or used by individuals at your organization. This can be as simple as an illegal software download or sharing of software licensing.

#7 – CYBERCRIME

Cybercrime is a crime that involves a computer and a network, which can threaten an individual, an organization, or a nation's security or financial health. The most continuously used cybercrime technique is phishing, the attempt to obtain sensitive information or data, such as passwords, by disguising oneself as a trustworthy entity in an electronic communication *(e.g., an email).* Other types of cybercrimes include hacking, unwarranted surveillance, or money laundering.

To counteract cybercrimes, well-designed cybersecurity measures to protect computers, networks, and data, need to be put in place. Advanced tools should be used for detecting and removing malware. Operating systems should be up to date and patched regularly to prevent breaches. Confidential, proprietary, and sensitive information should always be transmitted securely.

Internal auditors that practice **TEA** ensure that all of the above is in place and that any cybersecurity red flags are identified and immediately addressed. They ensure network access is limited and secure, firewalls are impenetrable, passwords policies are strong and enforced, and robust data backup and restore strategies are in place. And they ensure there are effective cybersecurity policies governing the implementation of effective safeguards.

#8 - Cryptocurrency

In *"simple" (if you can call it that)* Wikipedia terms, cryptocurrency is a digital asset designed to work as a medium of exchange wherein individual coin ownership records are stored in a ledger existing in a computerized database. There is no physical form *(i.e., paper money)* and it is not issued by a central banking authority.

Blockchain is the technology behind the existence of cryptocurrency; the decentralized ledger of all cryptocurrency transactions. And Bitcoin, the other term you most likely are familiar with, is the most well-known type of cryptocurrency.

Why in the world am I giving you this quick terminology lesson? Because as our society continues to go cashless, these are terms every internal auditor needs to be familiar with. Whether your organization begins dealing in cryptocurrencies or interacts with organizations that do, it is important to stay abreast of what may be coming and the risks associated with its use.

One of the major risks associated with the use of cryptocurrencies is that they are meant to be pseudonymous and may be very difficult for auditors to recognize when a transaction involves fraud, illegal acts, or related-party transactions. The main goal for TEA is to ensure the proper specialized knowledge and competency exists within your organization and on your internal audit team to define and review cryptocurrency risks, processes, and controls.

Wow. Need a break?

That was a lot of potential ethical risks in current or future technology. Don't let it overwhelm you. Chances are your organization is only impacted by a few of them today. But the overall point is that one day soon organizations may be impacted by all of them and the sooner internal auditors can analyze the ethics, fraud, and risk impact, the more value internal audit will add to the organization's ability to advance technologically in an ethical way.

You officially made it through Step One: Plan and Think Like a Fraud Examiner... on to Step Two...

****

Step Two: Execute Like an Investigative Journalist

"Where were the auditors?"
– Too many people to cite

Why are auditors rarely mentioned in organization frauds or ethical crises, except for what they *failed* to uncover? Well, the answer may be:

1) They are working on the wrong things *(low red flag/ethical risks),*

2) They are not taking the right approach to what they are working on *(audit processes),* or

3) They do not have the proper qualities to do the work *(courage and grit).*

The previous section covered the first answer – how internal auditors can better focus on the right things by *Planning and Thinking Like a Fraud Examiner.*

And the last section is going to cover the third answer – the qualities need to be effective *Total Ethical Auditors.*

But this section *(and the next)* will focus on the second answer – how internal auditors need to approach their work. Starting with how to *Execute Like an Investigative Journalist.*

Let's start with some basic definitions:

Investigative Journalism – *"A form of journalism in which reporters deeply investigate a topic of interest or importance such as serious crimes, political corruption, or corporate wrongdoing."*

Contrast that with:

Internal Auditing – *"An independent, objective assurance and consulting activity designed to add value and to improve an organization's operations."*

The difference to me seems to be the *focus.*

Internal auditors typically follow the sacred annual audit plan, year after year, examining the same organization activities and records, uncovering the same vanilla issues, and, often, writing very similar reports.

Investigative journalists dig into issues of importance *(red flags)* based on the depth of various sources of information, forming and testing a hypothesis, and performing rigorous fact checking and data analysis *(think data analytics).*

It is reported that all investigative journalists share a few common traits. Let's see how these traits match up with internal auditors...

- ✓ Good investigative journalists are on a mission for change and they take a stance; they are not just reporting what happened. *Are auditors simply reporting the "news" from the past or are they taking a stance on changing the future?*

- ✓ Good investigative journalists have a passion for truth and justice, to serve their audience with stories that matter, no matter the cost. *Do auditors have the same passion and purpose to find the truth for the organizations they serve?*

- ✓ Good investigative journalists have curiosity and initiative. It's a tip here and a source there. They take the initiative, track down the facts, and get the story before someone else does. *Are auditors listening to all the tips and finding the problems before someone else, inside or outside the organization, does?*

✓ Good investigative journalists dig deep and back up stories with research, sources, and facts. They analyze all the facts in a way that readers can easily understand the issues. It takes a lot of work. *Are auditors doing the hard work, analyzing data effectively, and communicating the results appropriately?*

✓ Good investigative journalists think logically, are well-organized, and disciplined. There's never enough time to meet deadlines, yet they still do. *Are auditors efficient and effective in producing a product of high value in a timely manner to their organizations? Or is the work too late and too costly with little value?*

✓ Good investigative journalists are flexible and willing to go wherever the story takes them. Based on questions, they often re-think the mission and re-direct their research. *Do auditors follow their annual audit plan whether it adds value or not? Or are they continuously updating the scope of their work?*

✓ Good investigative journalists have great collaborative and communication skills. They have the contacts, networks, and necessary relationships to be effective. *Do auditors have the essential communication and relationship skills to get the information they need on the high risks?*

Perhaps you have some hard questions to answer.

Now let's take a look at some examples of stories that were *"uncovered"* by investigative journalists – some that we've already mentioned in the book.

****

There is GardaWorld, where major health and safety risks exist. The risks were well known to many within the Garda organization, and although some did attempt to expose the unsafe practices that caused many injuries and death, the full story finally broke wide open when the Tampa Bay Times reporters pursued the story, did the research, obtained and analyzed the facts, and visibly exposed the unsafe practices and conditions that put employees and the general public at risk.

Their great investigative reporting can be seen at:

https://projects.tampabay.com/projects/2020/investigations/garda-world/armored-trucks/

****

Then there was the Johns Hopkins All Children's Hospital in St. Petersburg, Florida. A newspaper reporter learned that physicians at the hospital had left a surgical needle in a baby's chest. The reporter had gotten an earlier tip that there were some unusual personnel moves such as top physicians being dismissed. The hospital was not forthcoming with information. So, the reporter began an investigation into data from other sources involving children's surgeries. The results were stunning; the death rate of heart surgeries at the hospital was three times the statewide average.

After a series of newspaper articles, major personnel changes were made at the hospital and federal and state investigations began, resulting in serious findings, huge settlements, and corrective actions. There was no mention of internal auditors or external regulators until the story broke. But, of course, they all arrived in force after the fact.

See the investigative journalists' reporting at:

https://projects.tampabay.com/projects/2018/investigations/he artbroken/

****

Then there is John Carreyrou from the Wall Street Journal (WSJ) that exposed the fraud at the startup blood testing company, Theranos. Founder and CEO Elizabeth Holmes was mentioned in the *(Un)Ethical Organization* chapter.

The WSJ had previously published an article about Theranos in the early years of the company. Claims made by Holmes at that time were taken on face value. Over time, due to the secretiveness of the company, there were suspicions that the technology was not working. The suspicions were confirmed when a tip arrived at the WSJ from a former Theranos employee. The tip – the new technology claims of the company were a fraud. After many interviews and much digging, Carreyrou broke the story wide open. The blood tests were faulty, the company crumbled, and investors lost hundreds of millions of dollars.

In the case of Theranos, there seemed to have been no internal or external audits – only some insubstantial reviews by external consultants *(hired by Walgreens, a Theranos customer)* and after the fact regulatory reviews. But there was a Board made up, at one time or another, of former U.S. Secretaries of State, a former U.S. Secretary of Defense, and several former CEOs of major corporations. A few had science and medicine backgrounds but most didn't. None exercised the oversight necessary to prevent the fraud.

For the rest of the story about the rise and fall of Theranos, read Carreyrou's book, *Bad Blood*, or the articles in the WSJ at:

https://www.wsj.com/articles/theranos-has-struggled-with-blood-tests-1444881901

****

Investigative reporting involves a set of techniques including finding the critical documents and following the paper trail, interviewing sources and following the people trail, and analyzing data and following the electronic trail. And journalists often go to the scene to investigate firsthand; they don't hide behind their desks. *Do your internal auditors spend time in the field, or do they hide behind their desks?*

When an investigative journalist writes a report or publishes a story, it represents a significant investment in time and other resources. It involves gathering information based on the resourcefulness and initiative of the journalist, and it results in revealing information not otherwise known that is critical to the public. *Here's another tough question: How do your internal audit reports compare? Do they contain information critical to your organization?*

Maybe, just maybe, if internal auditors took a more focused, investigative approach to high risk issues, it would result in more meaningful, impactful internal auditing. Auditors, it's time to *Execute Like an Investigative Journalist...* and find the story at your organization, first.

On to Step Three...

****

STEP THREE: MITIGATE LIKE A COACH

What's an internal audit function to do when there are leaders with little integrity motivated by personal greed, accounting processes filled with financial engineering and shortcuts, weak or nonexistent board members and oversight, and/or external auditors that are compromised by conflicts of interest?

Unfortunately, even if we are the best fraud examiner or investigative journalist that exists, there are just not enough resources to catch all individuals that exhibit unethical behavior – those that lie, cheat, or steal in one form or another. No system of governance, risk management, controls, or traditional internal audit programs can weed out all the fraudsters or put every culprit in jail.

So, the only practical answer is to mitigate unethical behavior by coaching individuals, leaders, and organizations in ways that will prevent unethical conduct before it occurs. As deception expert Timothy Levine says:

> *"...the human solution to the problem of deception is deterrence."*

And as I say in *Total Quality Auditing,*

> *"Internal auditors need to stop catching and start coaching."*

So, the TEA solution to deterring unethical conduct is to start *coaching, consulting, counseling, mentoring, communicating, and training.*

It may seem easier said than done but there are some concrete things that proactive internal audit functions can do. The priorities, actions, and processes that were outlined in the *Ethical Leadership* and *Ethical Organization* chapters are where you need to begin to *Mitigate Like a Coach:*

> ➢ Ensure proactive compliance with the spirit, letter, and intent of laws and regulations.

> ➢ Advise leaders on properly balancing the interests of all stakeholders, not just shareholders.

> ➢ Assist leaders in clearly stating and regularly communicating ethical values and ensure ethical values are executed above all others.

> ➢ Ensure realistic expectations are set and reasonable resources are provided to accomplish objectives.

> ➢ Train those involved in personnel selection, promotion, and development processes to ensure the hiring and advancement of ethical employees.

> ➢ Assist in the establishment and communication of organization standards of conduct and ensure the administration and enforcement is fair and effective.

> ➢ Be aware of and monitor conflicts of interest situations and ensure conflicts are eliminated and dealt with ethically.

> ➢ Eliminate the use of FGBKs *(favors, gifts, bribes, and kickbacks)* at your organization.

> ➢ Advocate for zero tolerance for unethical conduct.

> ➢ Train employees and leaders regarding their ethics-related responsibilities and ethical decision-making as

well as their accountability for reporting unethical conduct.

➤ Evaluate and investigate whistleblower complaints and ensure appropriate corrective action is taken and protect whistleblowers from retaliation. *Thirty-six percent of whistleblowers report that they suffered some form of retaliation for reporting the misconduct. Make sure your organization loves their whistleblowers.*

➤ Advise in the development and administration of programs to recognize and reward ethical behavior.

➤ Raise awareness of professional codes of conduct where applicable and ensure compliance with the codes. Monitor and investigate deviations from the professional codes for appropriate corrective action.

➤ Advocate organization structures that provide ethical checks and balances for decision-making.

➤ Conduct periodic surveys, individual, and group meetings to obtain feedback regarding ethical issues and breaches. Provide feedback to leaders and board members. *Good coaches want feedback from their players.* Ensure appropriate corrective action is taken to permanently fix or eliminate the potential for ethical issues, wherever possible.

"Inspection with the aim of finding the bad ones and then throwing them out is too late, ineffective, and costly."
– W. Edwards Deming

It is time internal auditors are not just inspecting and catching past organizational *(ethical or otherwise)* mistakes; it is too late, ineffective, and costly. It is time to have a TEA mindset of

Mitigating Like a Coach, coaching unethical behavior out of our organizations.

On to the last step, which is essential for accomplishing the previous three steps. Step Four...

****

STEP FOUR: BE A TOTAL ETHICAL AUDITOR

Internal auditors should be facilitators of the law abiding, ethical relationships between the organization's board of directors, executives, and management and all stakeholders: regulators, communities, partners, suppliers, contractors, employees, customers, and shareholders.

Internal audit should be a leader in promoting honesty and transparency by all, compliance with organization ethical values and standards of conduct, and adherence to applicable professional ethical conduct standards. They should be mitigating ethical risks and reporting on and investigating ethical breaches. And above all, they need to display general good ethical citizenship at the organization.

In order to perform these duties, internal auditors need to follow the highest standards of professional ethical conduct themselves. As I mentioned early on in this chapter, the IIA Code of Ethics four cornerstones are:

Integrity – The integrity of internal auditors establishes trust and thus provides the basis for reliance on their judgment.

Objectivity – Internal auditors exhibit the highest level of professional objectivity in gathering, evaluating, and communicating information about the activity or process being examined. Internal auditors make a balanced assessment of all the relevant circumstances and are not unduly influenced by their own interests or by others in forming judgments.

Confidentiality – Internal auditors respect the value and ownership of information they receive and do not disclose information without appropriate authority unless there is a legal or professional obligation to do so.

Competency – Internal auditors apply the knowledge, skills, and experience needed in the performance of internal audit services.

The IIA Code of Ethics is just fine for traditional internal audit processes for assurance and consulting work. However, in order to focus on the *serious ethical risks* at an organization, I believe there are a few heightened and added qualities an internal auditor will need.

Yes, you will still need the highest personal and professional *integrity* along with the right audit *competencies*. But you will also need a healthy amount of *skepticism, grit,* and *courage.* Each of these five attributes play a critical role in becoming the *Total Ethical Auditor.*

THE ETHICAL AUDITOR

"On matters of style, swim with the current, on matters of principle, stand like a rock."
– Thomas Jefferson

The ethical auditor fully embraces the professional IIA Code of Ethics cornerstones of integrity, objectivity, and confidentiality. But they are also well grounded in *Ethical Anchors* from the past and present, and they have spent time developing personal ethical values and standards of personal ethical conduct. They understand and support organizational ethics values and standards as well.

The ethical auditor is independent and objective in all audit activities, always without personal bias, and rarely conflicted. When conflicts do arise, the ethical auditor puts personal and professional ethical standards first, even when they could be adversely impacted personally or professionally.

The ethical auditor is more interested in eulogy virtues than resume virtues *(thank you, David Brooks)*. And the ethical auditor takes to heart ethical leadership examples described in this book.

And finally, the ethical auditor maintains confidentiality unless there is a legal, professional, or *ethical* obligation to disclose information – *with ethical being a very important distinction.*

For the *Total Ethical Auditor*, personal and professional ethics are beyond reproach – a very high standard.

****

THE COMPETENT AUDITOR

> *"Whatever you are, be a good one."*
> – Abraham Lincoln

The IIA rules of conduct for competency states: *"Internal auditors shall engage only in those services for which they have necessary knowledge, skills, and experience."*

While I agree that competence includes having the knowledge, skills, and experience, I also believe it means being responsive to customer needs, building positive rapport, communicating effectively, being lean and efficient, and problem solving to earn respect. The competent auditor knows the continuous improvement of each of these qualities *(both technical and "soft" qualities)* is required in order to make the greatest impact. And the competent auditor sets stretch goals and is committed to exceeding expectations.

But above all of that, the competent auditor assumes a leadership role in establishing and maintaining an ethical culture. The competent auditor focuses their attention on the crucial high risk ethical issues and provides permanent solutions to reduce the risks. They ensure processes are in place to minimize ethical risks and maximize ethical conduct.

The mission is clear for the *Total Ethical Auditor* – lead all to more ethical ends through ethical means.

****

THE SKEPTICAL AUDITOR

"Never think you have seen the last of anything."
– Eudora Welty

The skeptical auditor takes to heart the messages of the *Ethical Mirage* chapter and professors like Ariely, Bazerman, Levine, Messick, Tenbrunsel, and the many others who have investigated the connections between ethics and behavior.

The skeptical auditor knows the clear conclusions: that individuals are not as ethical as they think they are, *and* individuals have a difficult time detecting deception. Therefore, the skeptical auditor knows the necessary characteristics needed to be effective in their work.

They know to guard against Levine's *"truth-default"* theory and his research-based conclusions that indicate human beings *"accept virtually all of the communication messages... as honest."* They don't fall into the trap of believing what they are told, a pretty dangerous trap if internal auditors are to be effective – especially in identifying unethical conduct.

Total Ethical Auditors know that understanding ethics, behavioral and communication research, and being professionally skeptical is a necessity in the audit profession.

****

THE GRITTY AUDITOR

"Our potential is one thing.
What we do with it is quite another."
– Angela Duckworth

Angela Duckworth, professor of psychology at the University of Pennsylvania, wrote the book *Grit: The Power of Passion and Perseverance*. Duckworth defined the term grit and conducted research validating the importance of grit and the positive relationship between grit and success. And after reading it, I immediately began teaching internal auditors how to *"audit with grit."*

Those with grit have the passion to add value in everything that they do, to make a permanent difference. The gritty auditor has a passion for auditing; they enjoy the work, but more importantly, they believe in the bigger purpose of auditing and its impact on the success of their organization. They are the first to spot key risks as well as improvement opportunities.

The gritty auditor also has the perseverance to overcome any obstacle. They persist through difficult conversations and ensure effective completion of high risk audits.

The gritty auditor sees every ethical breach as an opportunity to investigate, understand causes, correct processes, educate, and change behavior. They dig to find the facts, and they analyze and present those facts, even in challenging situations. They don't back down.

Internal auditors are placed in situations that can be contradictory; they have a requirement to be independent but build good relationships; they have a need to be skeptical but collaborative; they need to be critical of the past while bringing insights into the future.

To see all things to an ethical and successful end requires a lot of grit from *Total Ethical Auditors.*

****

THE COURAGEOUS AUDITOR

> *"The truth of the matter is that you always know the right thing to do. The hard part is doing it."*
> – Gen. H. Norman Schwarzkopf

I saved the most important characteristic of *Total Ethical Auditors* for last. Courage, as defined by the Merriam-Webster dictionary is the *"mental or moral strength to venture, persevere, and withstand danger, fear, or difficulty."* If you ask me, it takes courage to display any of the codes of ethics principles we previously discussed: ethics, integrity, objectivity, confidentiality, competency, skepticism, or grit. I mean, without the *courage* to display your integrity *(or insert any other quality here),* the principles are practically meaningless.

All internal *(and external)* audit activities take *"mental and moral strength."* The profession can be quite competitive and difficult, full of managing conflicting interests and those who are willing to achieve ends by any means.

As I have noted already, major frauds generally involve senior members of management. Business interests sometimes conflict with the interests of ethical conduct through the eyes of some leaders. Ethical risks are often significant, and consequences can be disastrous – lives, livelihoods, and reputations are at stake.

So, the courageous auditor is on front line of promoting ethics awareness in an effort to mitigate ethical risks and prevent unethical conduct. They are engaged in proactive efforts to implement processes and controls to sustain ethical conduct.

The courageous auditor speaks and reports the truth to auditees, management, executives, and board members, even when they don't want the bad news. And courageous auditors let everyone know that truth is expected in return.

The courageous auditor carries the ethical banner when no one else is willing to. They do what is right *even if* it costs them a friendship, a client, or their job.

Total Ethical Auditors know *right* from *wrong* and they have the courage to *do things the right way, the first time.*

****

You have officially made it to the end of this chapter and know what it takes to practice TEA:

Think and Plan like a Fraud Examiner

Execute like an Investigative Journalist

Mitigate like a Coach

Be A Total Ethical Auditor

This is the Total Ethical Auditing Proposition.

Stick around for a few concluding comments from yours truly...

EXPLORE TOTAL ETHICAL AUDITING

The following are questions for internal auditors who want to be *Total Ethical Auditors:*

Do you understand the difference among traditional internal auditing, Total Quality Auditing®, and Total Ethical Auditing?

What are the four steps to becoming a Total Ethical Auditor?

What does "plan and think like a fraud examiner" mean?

What are the three factors of the Fraud Triangle Assessment?

What are the four factors of the Risk Impact Assessment?

How do disingenuous leaders and boards impact organization ethics?

Why is ethical finance and accounting leadership critical to organization ethics?

What are the potential accounting process red flags?

What are the ethical dangers of aggressive compensation and incentive plans?

How does technology impact ethics?

What are the areas of technology with the greatest ethical risks?

How do an organization's standards of conduct include ethics?

How can you influence the environment and behaviors at your organization?

What does "execute like an investigative journalist" mean?

How can an auditor "mitigate like a coach?"

What are the five qualities of a Total Ethical Auditor?

AUTHOR'S CONCLUDING COMMENTS

"Truth is the only safe ground to stand on."
– Elizabeth Cady Stanton

UNFORTUNATELY, IT SEEMS to be a sad time in our society when it comes to trust. The world appears to be heading down a path that is more and more impersonal and competitive. In the past, religion played a prominent part of our lives, reminding us one way or another of the importance of moral and ethical conduct. But those traditional moral and ethical standards and benchmarks seem to be gradually disappearing.

And it seems that increasingly people are torn between self-interest *(that a bit of cheating or lying can enhance)* and the innate desire to view ourselves as honorable human beings; as

Socrates said, *"to endeavor to be what you desire to appear."* We want our cake and eat it too.

The social pressures are great, and our defenses are weak. There is pressure to achieve material success. There is pressure to cut corners, to fudge the truth, and please our bosses.

But look on the bright side: Evidence shows that although many lie, cheat, and steal *a little,* very few lie, cheat, and steal *a lot.* And there are many *Ethical Anchors* that can help in our efforts to improve ethically, especially for the many of us that need only *"a little"* help along the path.

Throughout this book, I have compiled many, many, great individual perspectives, thoughts, and quotes while sprinkling in my own. I want to personally honor and thank Bogle, Bok, Blanchard, Brooks, Huntsman, Maxwell, Peale, and Sandel for their ethical wisdom and for laying the groundwork to becoming *The Everyday Ethicist.* And extra credit to Benjamin for a school assignment well done, reminding us, much like Huntsman, to never forget those values we learned as children.

Yes, I pointed out lots of failures in leadership along the way, but remember the ethical leadership models of Bogle, Cathy, Cloud, Horowitz, North, Tubman, Roosevelt, Vestager, and Birx. We have them to thank for showing us the path to becoming *The Everyday Ethical Leader.*

Yes, there have been plenty of organizations that have failed ethically, but for every failure there have also been many with values, standards, behaviors, and processes that support and sustain an ethical culture for all stakeholders. Chick-fil-A, Wegmans, Vanguard, and A. A. Peck and Sons General Store are just a few that showed us the way to becoming *The Everyday Ethical Organization.*

When you recall this book, I want you to think of the positive examples of personal, leadership, and organizational integrity and ethical decision-making. I want you to remember the individuals who focused not on what they *could* do, but on what they *should* do. Because ethics, whether as an individual, a leader, or an organization, is really just about doing what is *positive and right.*

It's about understanding that character is earned through a long record of ethical decision-making.

It's about knowing that trust is earned by keeping your commitments and always sticking to your ethical values.

It's about never compromising integrity, no matter the cost or consequence.

It's about being proud of the fact that you can be counted on to speak the truth under all circumstances.

It's about being honored to have your actions on the front page of the paper or included in a book about ethics.

It is time to build a new crowd of Everyday Ethicists to chant Deming's pronouncement, *"We are here to make another world."*

We all have the power within us to be honest and ethical. We all have the power to influence others through the methods and means described throughout the book. And, we all have the power to refuse to accept others duplicity because we have the choice with whom we associate.

Leaders and organizations must accept the challenge of creating climates that are conducive for ethical conduct. They must provide the incentives and support to be ethical while vocally discouraging unethical conduct. They must lead, mentor, and train in such a way that there is no doubt about ethical expectations.

Lastly, I highly encourage everyone to ask themselves a few really important questions at the end of every day:

❖ *What examples of integrity and character did I display?*

❖ *What ethical weaknesses do I still need to overcome?*

❖ *Can I look myself in the mirror and know I was ethical?*

To help with that last question, here is a great poem to save...

The Man In The Glass
Peter Dale Wimbrow Sr.

When you get what you want in your struggle for self
And the world makes you king for a day
Just go to the mirror and look at yourself
And see what that man has to say.

For it isn't your father, or mother, or wife
Whose judgment upon you must pass
The fellow whose verdict counts most in your life
Is the one staring back from the glass.

He's the fellow to please – never mind all the rest
For he's with you, clear to the end
And you've passed your most difficult, dangerous test
If the man in the glass is your friend.

You may fool the whole world down the pathway of years
And get pats on the back as you pass
But your final reward will be heartache and tears
If you've cheated the man in the glass.

Work to grow your integrity and character.

Work to look honestly at yourself in the mirror.

Work at *doing things the right way the first time...*

and every time.

THIS IS MY FINAL ETHICS PROPOSITION.

APPENDIX

EXHIBIT I

THE EVERYDAY ETHICIST CONTRACT

√ Recognize everyone is vulnerable to unethical behavior.

√ Develop your own personal value statement and ethical code of conduct.

√ Focus on your actions and the effect they have on others. Do no harm to others.

√ Practice writing down thoughts to get a clear, developed plan for conduct and actions.

√ Visualize defending you actions in front of a judge.

√ Imagine an article on the front page of the Wall Street Journal describing your actions.

√ Project ethical challenges into future situations and pre-commit to intended ethical choices.

√ Judge your own ethical decisions the way you would judge others.

√ Review critical ethical decisions and alternative actions with personal mentors or professional colleagues and/or trusted advisors before acting.

√ Make decisions as if you had trusteeship, stewardship, or fiduciary responsibility for others.

√ Meet or exceed your commitments and do not overcommit or exaggerate.

√ Commit to serve the best interests of clients, in particular, and society, in general.

√ Resolve any conflicts between business interests and personal interests in the favor of others.

√ Let every ethical crisis develop your character and strengthen your resolve to do the right thing.

√ Be proud of your integrity and be a model for ethical conduct. Walk the talk.

√ Build your most important ethical assets of courage, honesty, and humility.

√ Treat others better than they treat you. Pay it forward.

√ Speak truth. Speak up. Speak truth to power.

√ Don't compromise your integrity at any cost.

EXHIBIT II
CHECKLIST FOR ETHICAL DECISION MAKING

PERSONAL

> Does the decision do no harm to others?

> Is the decision consistent with your personal values and conduct standards?

> Is the decision based on truth, honesty and facts?

> Are you resolving conflicts between your interests and others in favor of others?

LEGAL

> Is the decision consistent with applicable federal, state, and local laws?

> Is the decision in compliance with agency regulations?

PROFESSIONAL

> Is the decision consistent with the spirit and intent of applicable professional standards and values?

> Would your trusted professional colleagues approve of the decision?

> Is the decision consistent with applicable trusteeship and fiduciary standards?

ORGANIZATIONAL

> Is the decision consistent with organization values?

> Is the decision consistent with organization standards of conduct?

> Does the decision represent the interests of your customers?

> Does the decision represent the interests of *all* stakeholders?

COMMON SENSE

> - Would your parents approve of the decision?

> - Would your pastor, priest or rabbi approve of the decision?

> - Are you being a good steward for others' interests?

> - Are you honoring your commitments?

> - Are you doing the right thing that will serve as a model for ethical behavior for others?

> - Do you speak up when you see unethical behavior?

Exhibit III

The Everyday Ethical Leader Checklist

- Maintains high ethical personal and professional standards for self and inspires others to do likewise.

- Establishes and communicates clear organization ethical values and put values above all else.

- Establishes ethical standards with accountability for personal conduct.

- Honestly serves all stakeholders' interests. Puts others interests above self-interest.

- Walks the *ethical* talk. Knows what you do is who you are.

- Honors commitments. A promise is a promise.

- Treats others with dignity and respect.

- Sets realistic goals and provides reasonable resources to accomplish the goals.

- Fosters open communications about ethical breaches with no retaliation.

- Deals with crises honestly and openly.

- Listens to the needs of others. Is empathetic and sensitive with courage to do what's right.

- Trusts others and gains the trust of the people they lead.

- Values character over personal wealth, fame, or power.

- Leads as if it is the family business.

EXHIBIT IV

ETHICAL VALUE STATEMENTS

Act with integrity; do what is right.
– Coca Cola

Delivering on our promises, doing what we say, and what is right.
– CVS

Continual success depends on a commitment to conduct business with honesty and integrity.
– Disney

Activities will be conducted to the highest ethical and professional standards.
– FedEx

Be honest, fair, and trustworthy in all activities and relationships.
– GE

Uphold the highest levels of business ethics and personal integrity in all types of transactions and interactions.
– Berkshire Hathaway

Enduring and heartfelt goodness is evident in all we do.
– Hershey

Conduct business with uncompromising integrity.
– Hewlett Packard

We act with integrity and show respect.
– Kellogg's

Set the example for each other and our stakeholders by being honest and fair.
– Nokia

Be honest: We're ethically, fiscally, and environmentally responsible.
– The Reputation Institute

Success is built on trust; trust starts with transparency.
– Salesforce

Acting with integrity and sound social norms.
– Toyota

Reputation is built on a legacy of unwavering commitment to ethical behavior.
– USAA

Do the right thing.
– Vanguard

Always act with integrity; lead with integrity and expect others to work with integrity.
– Walmart

Loyalty, Duty, Respect, Selfless Service, Honor, Integrity, and Personal Courage
– U.S. Army

EXHIBIT V

WORKPLACE ETHICS SURVEY

To take this anonymous survey, use your smart phone to scan the QR code below or visit:

https://survey.zohopublic.com/zs/ACB35h

Suggested Readings

THE FOLLOWING are books referenced throughout this book. Others relate to the subject material that I believe provide useful information and messages. *In the Heart of the Sea* by Nathanial Philbrick is included because it is the classic tale of ethical decisions under extreme adversity.

Aristotle, translated by W. D. Ross, (1908). *Nicomachean Ethics*. Pantianos Classics.

Bazerman, M. H., & Tenbrunsel, A. E. (2012). *Blind Spots*. Princeton, NJ. Princeton University Press.

Beauchamp, Tom L., & Childress, James F. (2001). *Principles of Biomedical Ethics*. New York, NY. Oxford University Press.

Bennis, Warren. (2009). *On Becoming a Leader*. Philadelphia, PA. Basic Books.

Biegelman, Martin T. & Bartow, Joel T. (2012). *Executive Roadmap to Fraud Prevention and Internal Control*. Hoboken, NJ. John Wiley & Sons, Inc.

Blanchard, Kenneth, & Peale, Norman Vincent. (1988). *The Power of Ethical Management*. New York, NY. William Morrow and Company, Inc.

Bogle, John C. (2005). *The Battle for the Soul of Capitalism*. New Haven, CT. Yale University Press.

Bogle, John C. (2009). *Enough.* Hoboken, NJ. John Wiley & Sons, Inc.

Bogle, John C. (2019). *Stay the Course.* Hoboken, NJ. John Wiley & Sons, Inc.

Bok, Sissela. (1978). *Lying: Moral Choice in Public and Private Life.* New York, NY. Patheon Books.

Bok, Sissela. (2010). *Exploring Happiness.* New Haven, CT. Yale University Press.

Brooks, David. (2015). *The Road to Character.* New York, NY. Random House.

Brooks, David. (2019). *The Second Mountain: The Quest for a Moral Life.* New York, NY. Random House.

Carnegie, Dale. (1936). *How to Win Friends and Influence People.* New York, NY. Pocket Books.

Carreyrou, John. (2018). *Bad Blood.* New York, NY. Knopf Doubleday Publishing.

Cathy, S. Truett. (2002). *Doing Business the Chick-fil-A Way.* Decatur, GA. Looking Glass Books.

Ciocchetti, Cory. (2018). *Inspire Integrity.* New York, NY. Morgan James Publishing.

Cloud, Henry. (2006). *Integrity.* New York, NY. HarperCollins Publishers.

Collins, James C. (2001). *Good to Great.* New York, NY. William Collins.

Covey, Stephen R. (1989). *The Seven Habits of Highly Effective People*. New York, NY. Simon and Schuster.

Covey, Stephen M.R. & Merrill, Rebecca R. (2006). *The Speed of Trust*. New York, NY. Free Press.

Dalio, Ray. (2017). *Principles of Life and Work*. New York, NY. Simon & Schuster.

Deming, W. Edwards. (1994). *The New Economics*. Cambridge, MA. The MIT Press.

Deming, W. Edwards. (1982). *Out of the Crisis*. Cambridge, MA. The MIT Press.

Dobrin, Arthur. (2002). *Ethics for Everyone*. New York, NY. John Wiley & Sons, Inc.

Drucker, Peter. (1967). *The Effective Executive*. New York, NY. Harper Business Essentials.

Duckworth, Angela. (2016). *Grit: The Power of Passion and Perseverance*. New York, NY. Scribner Publishing.

Edmonds, David (2014). *Would You Kill the Fat Man*. Princeton, NJ. Princeton University Press.

Erven, Amanda Jo. (2019). *Total Quality Auditing*. Denver, CO. Four Aces Press.

Erven, Amanda Jo. (2019). *Our Choices on the Road of Life*. Denver, CO. Four Aces Press.

Fellers, Gary (1994). *Why Things Go Wrong*. Gretna, LA. Pelican Publishing Company.

Fountain, Lynn. (2016). *Ethics and the Internal Auditor's Political Dilemma.* Boca Raton, FL. CRC Press.

Fountain, Lynn. (2015). *Raise The Red Flag.* Altamonte Springs, FL. The IIA Research Foundation.

George, William. (2003). *Authentic Leadership.* San Francisco, CA. Josey-Bass.

George, Bill. (2015). *Discover Your True North.* Hoboken, NJ. John Wiley & Sons, Inc.

George, B., Craig, N., & Snook, S. (2015). *The Discover Your True North Fieldbook.* Hoboken, NJ. John Wiley & Sons, Inc.

Gladwell, Malcolm (2008). *Outliers.* Boston, MA. Little, Brown and Company.

Gladwell, Malcolm (2019). *Talking to Strangers.* New York, NY. Little, Brown and Company.

Hill, Napoleon. (1937). *Think and Grow Rich.* New York, NY. Random House Publishing.

Horowitz, Ben. (2019). *What You Do Is Who You Are.* New York, NY. Harper Collins Publishers.

Huntsman, Jon M. (2005). *Winners Never Cheat: Everyday Values We Learn as Children (But May Have Forgotten).* Upper Saddle River, NJ. Wharton School Publishing.

Huntsman, Jon M. (2009). *Winners Never Cheat: Even in Difficult Times.* Upper Saddle River, NJ. Wharton School Publishing.

Jansen Kraemer, Jr., Harry M. (2011). *From Values to Action.* San Francisco, CA. Josey-Bass.

Kanter, Rosabeth Moss. (1983). *Change Masters.* New York, NY. Simon & Schuster.

Kawasaki, Guy (2019). *Wise Guy.* New York, NY. Penguin Random House.

Levine, Timothy R. (2020). *Duped.* Tuscaloosa, AL, The University of Alabama Press.

Macy, Beth (2018). *Dopesick.* New York, NY. Little, Brown and Company.

Markopolos, Harry. (2010). *No One Would Listen.* Hoboken, NJ. John Wiley & Sons.

Maxwell, John C (2003). *There's No Such Thing as "Business" Ethics.* New York, NY. Hachette Book Group.

McLean, Bethany. & Elkind, Peter. (2003). *The Smartest Guys in the Room.* New York, NY. Penguin Group Publishing.

Messick, D. M. & Tenbrunsel, A. E. (1996). *Codes of Conduct* New York, NY. Russel Sage Foundation.

Peale, Norman Vincent. (1952). *The Power of Positive Thinking.* New York, NY. Touchstone Publishing.

Peters, T. & Waterman, R. (1982). *In Search of Excellence.* New York, NY. Collins Business Essentials.

Peters, Tom. (2018). *The Excellence Dividend.* New York, NY. Vintage Books.

Philbrick, Nathanial. (2000). *In the Heart of the Sea.* New York, NY. Viking Press.

Robbins, Anthony. (1986). *Unlimited Power.* New York, NY. Free Press.

Sandel, Michael J. (2009). *Justice.* New York, NY. Farrar, Straus,and Giroux.

Schilit, Howard M. & Perler, Jeremy (2010). *Financial Shenanigans.* New York, NY. McGraw-Hill.

Schwab, Charles. (2019). *Invested.* New York, NY. Random House.

Soltes, Eugene. (2016). *Why They Do It.* Philadelphia, PA. Perseus Books.

Stack, Ed. (2019). *It's How We Play The Game.* New York, NY. Simon & Schuster.

Taplin, Jonathon. (2017). *Move Fast and Break Things.* Boston, MA. Little, Brown and Company.

Willink, Jocko. (2020). *Leadership Strategy and Tactics.* New York, NY. St Martin's Press.

ABOUT THE AUTHOR

AMANDA "JO" ERVEN, CPA, CIA, CFE

Internal Audit Strategist

Management Consultant

Continuing Professional Education Trainer

Higher Education Professor

Keynote Speaker

Author

Amanda "Jo" is the President and Founder of Audit. Consulting. Education. LLC, a firm specializing in progressive Internal Auditing and management consulting and providing impactful CPE hours to organizations and individuals, globally.

Jo is a Certified Public Accountant (CPA), a Certified Internal Auditor (CIA), and a Certified Fraud Examiner (CFE) who pushes the envelope of traditional Internal Auditing. She believes audit should no longer be *"reactive"* and should focus on *"proactive,"* real value-add activities, melding quality and ethical behavior into the organization. Her trademarked approach to Internal Audit, *Total Quality Auditing*[®] (TQA) was published in both book and workbook format in 2019 (entitled *Total Quality Audit: How a Total Quality Mindset Can Help Internal Audit Add Real Value).* She provides in-person and virtual CPE trainings regarding her TQA techniques, which have already been successfully implemented by many organizations.

Personally, Jo is known for her proactive nature as well. After finding out she was positive for the breast and ovarian cancer gene mutation (BRCA1) in 2015, Jo underwent multiple preventative surgeries, including a double mastectomy in 2016. She believes knowledge is power and encourages others to take action in their lives. Jo's second book (also published in 2019 with an accompanying workbook), *Our Choices on the Road of Life,* begins with a look at her story and exploring how we can each make a choice to "embrace adversity." She also delivers several keynote presentations on our life choices, which have been called an *"epic experience."*

Jo has both her bachelor's and master's degrees in Accounting from the University of Georgia. She started her career in Public Accounting at one of the Big Four firms, experienced a traditional accounting role at a multinational corporation, and directed an Internal Audit function for ten years. She is also an Affiliate Faculty member at a State University in Colorado and has taught higher education courses including Principles of Accounting, Intermediate Accounting, Introduction to Business, and Internal Auditing.

Jo's experience includes advising management on a multitude of strategic initiatives, while providing ongoing recommendations for process and control improvements. She has designed SOX and other compliance programs, implemented audit management software suites, and has performed and managed financial, operational, and compliance audits for a multitude of industries, including oilfield services, agriculture, cannabis, transportation, insurance, retirement, investment, healthcare, higher education, and government. She has extensive risk assessment experience and focuses her efforts on what is critical for organizational success. She greatly enjoys working with her clients today on identifying and assessing their current and future risks.

Jo is an active member and instructor for the Colorado Society of CPAs (COCPAs) as well as a member of the Institute of Internal Auditors (IIA) and the Association of Certified Fraud Examiners (ACFE). Jo is currently serving as the Vice President of Academic Relations for the Denver Chapter of the IIA. Jo is also a Professional Member of the National Speakers Association, at both the state and national level. On a more personal note, Jo is a Leadership Committee member and active volunteer with Susan G. Komen Colorado.

Contact:

Jo@AuditConsultingEducation.com

www.auditconsultingeducation.com

Follow on LinkedIn:

https://www.linkedin.com/in/amanda-jo-erven-ace/

https://www.linkedin.com/company/audit-consulting-education-llc

COMMENTS ABOUT "JO"

"Jo is honest, bringing high integrity to all she does. She has the courage of her convictions and is one that always does the right thing."

"Ethics implies trust. Jo sets this tone because her career demonstrates she knows how to build it."

"Jo takes responsibility for her actions and believes in meeting or exceeding her commitments. Her behavior and results-oriented approach forms the foundation upon which people can place their trust."

"Jo is personable and approachable; she builds great relationships, treats others with respect, and earns the respect of others."

"Jo's authenticity, honesty, and candor are refreshing and genuine. Her ability to share her journey in a transferable way to a room of CPA's is a gift and an inspiration. Jo has enriched the lives of many."

"It is people like Jo who show the world that what may seem impossible or otherwise inescapable – isn't."

"Jo is a passionate and thoughtful leader who is not afraid to take action to drive positive change. Her ability to understand the needs of a business and to navigate and resolve difficult situations makes her an asset wherever she is. My career has greatly benefitted from the guidance and insight Jo has given me."

"Jo is a driven leader in her field and truly passionate in the development of others. She fosters a culture of constant improvement through mentorship and training to realize the highest potential from her team and bring value to clients and business partners. Her enthusiasm for learning and the development of others is second to none."

"Jo is a passionate leader who truly cares about her people. She is committed to her work and is dedicated to developing and mentoring her team. Jo is smart, efficient, and full of energy. She inspires the team and drives to achieve goals effortlessly."

"Jo teaches in a way that makes you want to learn from her. She is fun and creative and one of the best teachers I have EVER learned from!!!! She really helps me think!"

"The most valuable ethics information I have ever received in any ethics class I have ever taken... Brought up many topics for further pondering. Ethics is hard, not clear cut. Thanks Jo, for making such an important topic fun and informative."

"We invited Jo to present at our recent Ethics CPE event of almost 200 people. Jo made FOUR hours of ethics fun and engaging! Multiple people said as they were leaving that this ethics session was one of the best they've ever attended. Jo was a pleasure to work with!"

"You are articulating ideas that I've been trying to communicate for years, and I really appreciate the work you've done to propel the internal audit function towards the future and actually adding value."